the future of us

Ant Morse

Copyright © 2022 Adventa.tech
All rights reserved.
ISBN: 9798363921766

'Life moves pretty fast. If you don't stop and look around once in a while, you could miss it.'

Ferris Bueller

dedication

To all the people currently a little lost in the Digital Transformation storm.

My best friend and wife, Zoe, for her opinions, views, endless support, and my amazing book cover design.

My parents, who encouraged me to challenge the norm and give everything a go.

My mentor and friend, Steve Pluta, who introduced me to the 'art of the possible' many years ago.

CONTENTS

Acknowledgements   Pg. vii

Prelude.. Pg. 1

Chapter 1: Introduction .... Pg. 37

Chapter 2 Our Time in History..................... Pg. 44

Chapter 3: Why Our Time Will Be Different......... Pg. 79

Chapter 4: Understanding It All................... Pg. 123

Chapter 5: Impacts on Our Lives................... Pg. 143

Chapter 6: Future of Work......................... Pg. 148

Chapter 7: LAAS (Life As A Service) .... Pg. 185

Chapter 8: Staying Relevant....................... Pg. 206

Epilogue.. Pg. 250

Development Tool Set.............................. Pg. 254

Let's Connect..................................... Pg. 267

acknowledgements

To the thousands of colleagues and customers I've worked with over the years, too many to mention, but many of whom I'm privileged to now call friends.

Your views and opinions have shaped the pages of this book and I've loved our discussions along the way.

Every day's a school day, and I've learnt so much from the fortunate time I've had the pleasure of spending with some truly wonderful people

prelude

the story of scout

A light tapping on my wrist gently wakes me from sleep as a familiar voice softly calls out my name.

"Good morning, Ant. It's time to wake up."

Light gradually fills the room as a live image of a rising dawn projects itself onto my bedroom wall.

The tap is from my smartwatch, and the familiar voice is **Scout**, my Personal Virtual Digital Assistant. Scout guides me through practically every step of my day; it's hard to consider how I ever lived without her.

After our pre-agreed five-minute snooze, the tap and Scout's gentle voice return.

"Good morning, Ant, how are you on this – **sunny but cool ten degrees, slightly windy** – morning?

"The data from your watch suggests you had a reasonable sleep, but it could have been better – **watch data shows six hours of sleep recorded, thirty minutes of REM, and fifteen minutes awake** – so let's do a light workout this morning, and I'll look to move a few things around in your schedule today to help."

Scout's voice is channelled directly to me, using either my watch or any of the many connected speakers throughout the house, using spatial and directional audio so, in most cases, only I hear it.

There is also a speaker in my Smart Bed along with a heap of other technology that adjusts the temperature and firmness throughout the night, working in conjunction with the data from my watch to provide the maximum comfort and most optimal sleep possible. We sleep better in the future, though it comes at a price. But doesn't everything?

Raised from a ridiculously comfortable slumber, I now head to the bathroom and hear the familiar chime from the toilet, mid-flow, as it begins to process and analyse the contents, sending the data directly to my health application.

Health in the future is very proactive. Our National Health Service suffered unmanageable pressures during the Covid pandemic, which combined with our growing population and the ongoing challenges in recruiting and retaining staff across every area of the service.

Gradually, new technology was implemented into the service as prevention really is better than a cure and far more cost-effective long term. Governments across the globe launched services and digital applications that proactively focused on keeping people healthy. This was supported by a very active and willing private sector of independent health care providers who supplied advanced health monitoring solutions to the health-conscious among us in return for our monthly subscription as we moved from the National Health Service to 'Health As A Service'.

Fitness-tracker and smartwatch users moved from sharing their runs, rides, and hikes with friends on social media to sharing their activity data, coupled with readings from a range of home health devices (such as blood sampling and pressure devices and ECGs), with health providers that allowed both those in need and the 'worried well' a greatly improved remote and proactive health care service.

Dressed in shorts and a T-shirt with my water bottle in hand, I head to the spare room, ready for my virtual spin class. I place my Halo device on as I hop onto the saddle of our stationary bike, ready to enter my immersive digital world.

Halo is an Augmented Reality headset, similar in appearance and design to large ski goggles, or a floating fighter pilots' visor, held in place by a headband which houses the battery, speakers, and an array of small cameras and projectors that beam a range of content onto the Halo's clear screen, giving the wearer the impression that screens of information are floating in mid-air.

I blink as a quick flash of light carries out a retina scan and waits for me to say 'open'. The scan and my voice act as the dual factor security check to ensure it's me.

The information projected and the size of the screens we see vary depending on the application in use. For my cycling workout class this morning, I initially only see a small, tablet-sized screen appear to the left of my vision as the application loads and welcomes me to the class. The application is also slightly translucent, so I can still fully see my actual surroundings. The application view will gradually grow to fill the whole screen as the class begins. Simply saying 'stop', or double tapping any part of the Halo will close everything completely, returning me to the physical world in just a split second.

Augmented Reality (known as AR) grew in popularity as more things in our lives were digitised. The constant need to glance at our mobile devices or watches for notifications created the opportunity to introduce what I've called the 'Third Field of View', in which information and notifications are instantly projected into our current Field of Vision through Halos, or regular-looking glasses or contact lenses that have AR technology built into them. Regardless of the form factor, many simply refer to this technology as 'Glass'.

AR solutions were also designed to blur the lines between the physical and virtual worlds, often working in conjunction with traditional screens to enable content to pop from the screen in a richer, 3D, almost holographic, experience. This became huge in video-calling applications as it allows people in video calls to appear as though they are in the room with you.

There are many uses for this technology, from pop-up message notifications to information relevant to our local surroundings such as visiting towns and cities. So, as you'd expect, AR became big business for the tech giants who launched or relaunched AR hardware and solutions to ensure they stayed relevant in the battle for our attention and, of course, for the marketing opportunities this new Third Field of View delivered.

The other option for immersive interactions in the future comes from Virtual Reality (VR), a solution that allows us to leave the physical world completely through a headset that completely blocks out the physical world and immerses us fully into a truly digital world and environment where we can be whoever we want to be.

VR technology wasn't new, but it had previously struggled to find a compelling use case, so it took some time and development to deliver truly impressive solutions before people embraced it. And even then, it remained very niche and was used for a limited period or for specific tasks or applications.

AR and VR solutions combined are known as Extended Reality or Mixed (XR), and following significant investments and progress, XR quickly established itself as an essential part of our daily lives. Providing generations with a range of XR technologies and form factors that we'd have classed only a few years earlier as Sci-Fi. Yet now, they've become Now-Fi and have finally allowed us to truly 'travel without moving'.

Sci-Fi Becomes Now-Fi

XR Glass devices didn't win the battle to replace our trusty mobile devices, as many predicted. Our phones remain a very important companion in our digital futures, truly becoming the 'remote controls' to our digital lives. Sure, we looked at them less as watch and Glass projection technologies improved, but these devices simply connected via Bluetooth and used the processing power of our mobile in order to keep the size and weight of Glass devices low.

I have two 'go to' units; my comfy big-screen visor version for working from home, for entertainment, and for my workout class this morning, and my premium designer glasses, which I wear out and about. These look like regular glasses. However, the arms are slightly thicker to house the AR technology. The AR technology allows the glasses to project information only I can see into the top right-hand corner of the lens, though this tends to only be used for simple notifications, such as telling you who is calling or giving you directions or alerts of things around you in smart city or retail environments.

Back to the saddle, Scout hands over to Hope, my fitness instructor, who joins the session from her own home. While I have a slightly opaque image of her, it's clear that she is a real person.

"Good morning, class. I'm Hope, your instructor for today. It's great to see you all this morning! I hope you're all fit and well and ready for our ride today."

While others prefer the anonymity of a computer-generated instructor, I pay an increased monthly subscription to have a human instructor, rather than a virtual one, for some much-needed human interaction and conversation. I can quickly switch at any time for a computer-generated instructor should I not feel particularly social that day.

Hope is part of the growing number of Gig Workers who use their skills and experience to earn extra income or earn a living in a different way. Technologies have married supply and demand across pretty much every imaginable skill, which, coupled with changing societal attitudes towards how we earn a living, completely evolved the Future Of Work.

My fellow riders join from across the globe, appearing as either a real version of themselves or as avatars, often either because they do not have the right tech or simply out of personal preference. Considering I have just gotten out of bed, maybe I should have sent the digital version of myself instead! After all, we can be whoever we want to be – this is the gift of our digital world.

We say our hellos and collectively vote on a route, with voice translation services instantly translating everyone's speech into our native tongues as Hope shouts out:
"*OK, guys, let's get going with the warm-up. Let's get those legs moving, people!*"
Ah yes, I also paid for the sometimes annoying 'constant motivation' option when I signed up for my account. So, I'm likely to hear a lot more of this sort of thing throughout my ride. I call it 'Motivation As A Service', and I recall thinking it felt like a good idea at the time.

The Halo screen now changes from a small screen floating in my Field of Vision to a full-screen 360-degree view; every inch of the Halo is now filled with an immersive 3D image of our chosen route. This is where the AR becomes XR As I look left and right, the image adapts, allowing me to see both my fellow riders' avatars and the surroundings. If I turn and look behind me, the screen changes to show the actual view behind me in real time as well.

Gasping in awe at the beauty of the Italian lakes, today's chosen route, in my XR view, I remind myself not to get too carried away. I'm sitting on an expensive exercise bike in the spare room of my house in the north of England on a cool windy morning. Yet fake or not, this sure beats looking at my bedroom wall for the next thirty minutes.

My Halo screen is now set to 80% transparency, so I can see if someone comes into the room in my physical environment, but I can still focus fully on my class.

Following the growth of online fitness applications and services during the Covid lockdowns, we didn't all rush back to the gyms. We valued the convenience, flexibility, and anonymity of online fitness communities and found a happy medium between home and physical gym classes. We'd purchased Yoga mats, stationary bikes, treadmills, and free weights, joined local and global fitness communities, and focused far more time on our health.

We didn't give this up easily after the pandemic, with many finding it easier and more convenient to engage with like-minded people in virtual worlds as opposed to the sometimes quite intimidating gym environment. I went to the gym for many years and never really progressed from a brief nod and good morning to the same faces I saw many times a week – yet here, despite being with a bunch of strangers online who I will likely never meet in person, I find myself feeling more part of a group.

As we've been grouped based on our fitness levels and wider interests, with algorithms almost ensuring we have things in common, such as our sports interests, hobbies, or the industries we work in, we often find we have a lot in common. The application providers also appreciated our need for social interaction, providing time for people to chat in their applications if they choose to.

In this case, that time is built into the warm-up, and we chat as we start our ride, with today's topic being last night's football match. Someone shares details of a holiday they have just booked. I value this brief but essential human interaction in my digital world and I'm happy to pay for this feature.

Everyone is welcome in a virtual world where we can choose our participation levels. At a price, of course. You're noticing a theme, right? Yep. More and more things will be provided 'As A Service' in the Future Of Us.

With the ride well underway, we are now too immersed and out of breath to chat. I'm up out of the saddle and pushing hard as Hope snaps me back into the virtual space.

"Keep it going, guys! Ant, you're dropping back; dig deep and let's go with a big push for the last 500 and earn that fancy dinner later! On my count. Three... two..."

Shout-outs like this are personalised for each of us in the class; they are based on the data and information we are happy to share in this application. On this occasion, Hope knows I'm going out for dinner later as part of the data Scout has made available. I know it might sound a little fake, but this type of interaction happens throughout our days in the Future Of Us, and we accept its value over its authenticity.

There was something of a Data Revolution in the future as we reconsidered organisations' collection and usage of our data and, in turn, the value of our data to both organisations – and indeed ourselves – across the wider digital world.

The reality was that we'd been both knowingly and unknowingly surrendering heaps of detailed data to social media and application platform applications for many years. Yet we foolishly convinced ourselves that it was mainly secure and used appropriately. However, despite government regulations and rules on how our data was stored and used, we'd become a big product in the digital world.

'If you are not paying for the product, you are the product.'

So, rather than expecting others to protect and use our data responsibly, we took control of it ourselves using Artificial Intelligence (AI) and the new consumer data-sharing services that came to the market.

Government regulations with more transparent and tougher data policies were also introduced that, thanks to AI, allowed us to simply pull a report of all the data available on us from any organisation – allowing us to then choose what happens to it. In most cases, we deleted huge files of unnecessary data, asked after the purposes and intentions of that which remained, and finally, what the 'deal' was in return for any data beyond the basics that a company wished to keep.

As a result, organisations are now far more transparent with how they collate, store, and use our data. In turn, we agreed to offer relevant aspects of our own data, such as interests and shopping wish lists, in return for better services, discounts, and in some cases, hard cash. In the case of my fitness class, I chose to share with my instructor that I had a dinner date later that day as a point of reference to improve my experience. This information could have easily been that I was due to catch a train. Then, Hope may have wished me a safe journey.

This data exchange grew to enhance a mass of services in our lives; after all, providers' need for our data wasn't just financial. They needed our data in order to improve their services and solutions. A provider can't offer you a recommendation for a local restaurant or store if your location services are blocked. It needs to know where we are and what our preferences might be to give us the best recommendations.

The structure and workings of these solutions are nothing new; the big online retailers have used similar approaches for years.

The difference here is that we can choose what is or isn't stored and which brands we prefer to deal with, opening up an opportunity to engage with more local and small businesses in our region, not only with the big brands.

These applications only hold the data we allow, and we choose with who and when we share it; we can switch it on or off as we see fit. Saying 'I'd love a coffee' could instigate a search for the nearest coffee shop and using your pre-defined preferences such as type, or local, or big brand preferences would whittle it down instantly to a local offer, with the information instantly appearing on your phone or, of course, Glass device.

These data-sharing models moved way beyond shopping, with Innovators and Entrepreneurs bringing new applications across every sector built into our social interaction applications, capitalising on digital needs such as:

- **'Predict me':** Using the data we share to remember us and then push relevant services and offers to us.
- **'Entertain me':** Be it shopping or service, make it fun and interactive where possible.
- **'Love me':** Recognise and reward our loyalty.

"Great job, class. Enjoy your days. Ant, enjoy your dinner later, and I look forward to seeing you next time."

As we finish up the class, Scout now gives me a summary of my vitals and calories burned during the session. The data is simultaneously logged into my health portal. Did I do enough to earn the dessert, or is it the salad for me tonight?

"Hope you enjoyed your class, Ant. I'm preparing coffee now – **activate coffee machine** – I've started the shower for you – **start shower, thirty-eight degrees, five minutes** – I've adjusted the heating slightly, and we'll have a slightly longer breakfast this morning as I have a lot of updates to take you through – **turn thermostat to twenty-one degrees.**"

Scout is the next stage of Voice Assistance, and unlike Siri or Alexa, she is intelligent and goes beyond the basic features of today's intelligent Voice Services, which offer features such as a quick voice Internet search, switching lights on and off, and adjusting the heating.

Instead, solutions like Scout were designed to collate data and learn everything about us to improve themselves. From the things we search, the news we read, and the applications we use, even learning to detect when we might be tired or upset through our health stats and our tone of voice.

Scout is constantly collecting and processing data and proactively makes suggestions and decisions based on current and live changes in my data profile. She is also able to independently interoperate with the growing number of other smart applications and services.

I set and customised the initial parameters at the point of initial set-up. There were no typing or drop-down boxes; instead, Scout simply introduced herself, and we talked through a range of points and topics as Scout collated my answers and started to build my data profile of me.

There's no getting away from the fact that it feels odd talking to a computer-generated AI machine, but oddly, people kind of got used to it, and we soon took its benefits over the initial awkwardness. Once set up, I then have to choose the level of interaction and services… based on a wide range of options and monthly subscription models, of course.

From day one to day one hundred, Scout is a very different service. She enhances over time, constantly collating and processing the data I generate with the use of Machine Learning and Artificial Intelligence to make decision and interventions, which almost bring Scout to life.

The data remains ours, but the AI and learning model belong to the service providers, which see the battle to get these solutions just right as a major focus for the technology providers. The Glass solutions are only the access point; the AI behind Scout is the truly incredible part of the solution. Swapping these services to new providers is not something we do without very careful consideration.

And while it's a great addition to my life, we can also choose to switch Digital Assistants off as required, either to ensure privacy or simply just to take an occasional break from our digital life.

In practical reality, due to the efficiencies the service brings, Scout spends most of the day with me and combines with a mass of other applications I subscribe to; she ultimately manages my Life... As A Service.

• • •

In the shower, Scout returns.

"OK, Ant, so for the first part of your morning, we have a mix of video calls and project review meetings, followed by a great training course I've found for you. Then taking us up to lunch, we have a webinar you need to join with a wrap-up around 12:30 p.m. As always, we're working smarter, not harder today, Ant."

One of the most positive changes in the Future Of Us is the evolution of work. Using Digital Automation and AI technologies such as Scout, we realise that we can work far smarter. With attitudes to work already changing after the pandemic, the outdated nine to five model became rapidly redundant.

On reflection, we'd appeared to have 'sleepwalked' through our working lives and worked to a pattern originally designed to manage output in factories and production lines of the early 1900s. Time moved on, but we didn't appear to follow suit until the formation of new technology, a pandemic, and a subsequent societal shift opened our eyes to a new way.

The Great Resignation proved to be far from a short-term situation. People continued to closely evaluate how they lived and worked, making decisions based more on family balance over previous career ambitions.

Covid started an evolution of working practices that would have previously taken several decades to achieve.

People used their existing experience of working with technology during the pandemic to work in different ways, and collectively, we started a revolution of work that moved way beyond the technology itself and fundamentally changed the Future Of Work as we knew it.

Technology may have started the engine of the digital revolution, with innovative applications providing the fuel, but it was our changing societal attitudes that drove the journey of real transformation.

The best part of the Future Of Us is that there is less work!

"You have a dinner date with Zoe at 7 p.m. this evening, and we've checked the latest ratings via the Crowd and have found the perfect place for you both. It has some great reviews from your friends and wider Crowd networks – **Order Taxi for 6:45 p.m.** *–* and *don't forget to rate the restaurant and your experience afterwards in return for a discount on your next visit. But don't worry... I'll remind you later."*

Upon set up, I configured Scout to interoperate with my partner's AI assistance on certain tasks, such as checking diaries and schedules and comparing preferences. We set the levels of data sharing together, and we get the chance to intervene at various stages or to make any changes as we go, but as our Digital Assistants are using pre-defined preferences with Machine Learning systems constantly reviewing our collective data profiles, it's likely they will be making great choices for us, just by knowing us.

"Enjoy your shower, Ant. I've moved your first call to 9:15 a.m., and I'll prepare your schedule for review over coffee. I'll pass over now to the headlines, and some updates that I think will be of interest... and don't forget to wash behind your ears! **Play saved news articles and interest list highlights.**

*"Say '**skip**' or '**read later**' as required."*

A news reader's voice now takes over and guides me through the news headlines and some articles and stories that fall in line with pre-defined preferences and keywords that I chose upon setting up.

Scout also evolves her learning based on my recent reading and searches, using this to constantly search the Internet to find articles and stories that may be of interest to me or useful for my learning and career development.

Showered, dressed, and sat in my comfy chair with coffee in hand; I'm now ready for the day. Placing my Halo on again, Scout's face appears with a smile, and I re-enter my digital world.

Digitally synthetic or not, this next stage of Artificial Intelligence services changed our relationship with technology forever.

It began to move from very basic voice-to-text look-up solutions into a far more interactive and proactive two-way experience, almost conversational interactions.

However, it's still a long way off the claims and predictions of General Artificial Intelligence, where it would eventually become truly self-aware and conscious, almost coming alive and proactively thinking for itself without human intervention. Some experts suggest it will one day go way beyond that point and even surpass human intelligence. However, depending on your age, it's likely the majority of us won't see this become a reality in our lifetimes, if at all, but let's not rule anything out.

For now, our reality is that technology only does what we tell it to. Granted, it does it with some flair and an impression of consciousness, but it's still for the present day exactly as its title suggests... artificial.

But as I consider my day ahead, the line between Artificial or Self-Aware Intelligence blurs as solutions like Scout appear far cleverer than we fully appreciate by using a pre-defined set of rules, the data we let it use, and then the learning and decisions it makes along the way.

Take this morning as an example. Scout knew I would need to wake at a set time based on my diary, knew how much time to allow for my morning routine based on my first work appointment, and checked my watch data to play the appropriate messages based on the parameters of my sleep pattern. Scout chose my workout and even made a choice on the strength of my coffee based on the quality of my sleep, all while setting the temperature of the rooms she knew I was going to be in.

All these actions and rules are driven by those I chose and customised at set-up and tweak as I go, which collectively gives the appearance that she is actually self-aware.

"So, let's take a look at the day, Ant. We have twenty minutes before your first call, and I wanted to catch up on a few points."

As Scout appears in the middle of my Halo screen, she is surrounded by a number of almost translucent small summary boards suspended in mid-air. Imagine several floating tablet screens held up in front of you, which, just by holding your gaze on them, will come closer. We use our eyes as a mouse to quickly alternate between screens and apps.

As with my workout earlier, initially, all screens are slightly translucent, so I'm still aware of my physical surroundings. I could have chosen the fully immersive Virtual Reality option, but I like to stay partly in the real world for this part of my day, saving Virtual Reality for more immersive tasks and experiences.

Using this Third Field of View and floating applications is a far better experience than hunching over our phones or looking at single flat screens all day.

The screens show everything from tasks, messages, to-do lists, news headlines, and a range of notifications from social media and reminders of birthdays in my family and social networks.

"OK, Ant, your weekly work plans are in place. As a summary, the focus is mainly on a number of key projects you have in play and the accompanying calls and meetings to progress these. Current assessment is that I can do around 75% of the work for you, leaving just the more creative or challenging tasks to you.

"Checking the outstanding actions in your to-do list" – **which now appears centre screen** – "I've looked at what's required and who we need to help progress things. Some people have already responded, and I've updated accordingly – **display project update summary** – and others have requested more information that I'm unsure about. So, I've suggested and scheduled in some calls at convenient times for you all.

"On-screen now, you'll find the points I can't resolve for you with other Virtual Assistants in your to-do list. If you could review these and give directions, please, I will either respond or suggest follow-ups as well. We can work through in detail when you're ready."

We spend the next twenty minutes reading and talking through these tasks and incoming requests, progressing things in a quarter of the time it used to take.

This pattern of automation, our advanced learning, and access to incredible knowledge make for a super-efficient day, and the systems in play behind the scenes of Scout continually learn and adapt. They offer me daily adjustments with a few quick questions about how useful and efficient the system was, altering its service as needed to constantly improve it.

Scout is now pretty good at my job and learns as we work and pauses on any areas she is uncertain of, consulting me for guidance, but remembering for next time by using Machine Learning. Every response I make is recorded and contributes back into refining my Digital Assistant As A Service subscription.

As a result, we've just cleared what would be around four hours of work in the old world in twenty minutes.

Robots Taking Our Roles

As Artificial Intelligence progressed and began to take on more and more tasks for us, the question of whether Robots will take our jobs continued to surface.

Headlines suggested disruption on a grander scale as we started to see the automation of more and more roles and processes, both physical and digital. This was nothing new in the history of the Industrial Revolution, sure, but the pace of change underway was very different in our future; transformation happened far quicker than many could have imagined and, in turn, prepared for.

However, the reality for many was that while AI was pretty impressive in its ability, for the majority of roles, human skills were still required. Instead of replacing us, AI complemented us, and we worked alongside Robots as co-workers; this was termed 'CoBotics' and became a natural part of our lives.

I now guide Scout toward the responses I wish to make, allowing her to then form fuller replies instantly on my behalf. Scout has read all my previous communications; she understands my tone of voice, the constructs of my language, and even regional dialects. She will word responses accordingly, alternating the tone based on the relationships – from the more formal with customers and management to the less formal with closer colleagues and friends.

AI replies are also flagged to avoid any misinterpretations or etiquette misunderstandings.

"Ant, there are a few calls that you really don't need to be on today, I will use your Avatar and handle the Q&A from my knowledge bank. However, I will hold you on standby and provide either a playback summary or message you during the session if there is anything I can't answer. Or, if you prefer, you can just join for the Q&A?"

As our time in virtual and hybrid environments increased, so too did our need to improve how we presented ourselves in these digital worlds. Where possible, we presented a real image of ourselves via video, but where we couldn't be present, we sent a virtual version of ourselves in the form of an avatar.

Avatars are digital versions of us. They range from basic digital replicas using photos of us attached to basic figures to hyper-realistic Deep Synthetics, also known as Deep Fakes. With Deep Synthetics, we create ultra-realistic digital twins of ourselves from HD videos of us and our voicebanks. AI then uses this data to bring us to life, complete with facial expressions and shrugs of shoulders.

These are often so realistic that many would be hard-pressed to work out whether it's the real us or our avatars on-screen.

And while we might not fool everyone in passing these off as the true digital version of us, nor did we try to. They simply formed another presence option in future communication and our Future Of Work.

Nobody wants to see your ironing board, the pile of washing in the background, or the mass of bodies crammed onto a busy train carriage. Therefore, avatars became a popular choice to present the best versions of us in the future.

The Fuel of the Future – Connectivity

Not only did AI, Glass, and Avatar services rapidly develop and improve, but so too did the power to drive them, connectivity! Wires were complemented by Waves as 5G connectivity connected everything across our digital lives at speeds so fast we could read the emotions of our callers and interact in true real-time.

No more patchy coverage as people joined from trains or remote locations; everything works everywhere in the future.

the story of scout

The future is fast in many ways, and connectivity is its fuel. It allows us to almost realise the idea of travelling without moving, and it finally made the statement, 'work is something you do, and not somewhere you go' a reality.

The memory of our old world was never far away as we remembered the dreaded daily commute of chaotic early travels and making it home in darkness to kiss the foreheads of children already long asleep.

We collectively agreed that the commute to and from our offices every day was an inefficient use of time.

Furthermore, it was suggested that only 45% of our time pre-pandemic was actually spent on productive tasks when we were in the office. So, without the commute and distractions, the question for many was, "So what *is* the role of the office in the future?"

Well, our new solutions and shift in opinions on the role of the office didn't call an end to offices themselves. In fact, they still play a very important role in our working lives.

We did retain a small percentage of desks, allowing those that preferred to come into the office to do so. Even though working from home hit the headlines as a preference, it didn't work for many people – either due to not having a suitable space and environment or simply because they preferred the interaction and social engagement we only get from a physical office space.

So, we redesigned most of our office spaces from rows of desks into more collaborative and open shared spaces. We filled them with advanced audio and visual collaboration technologies and used the locations as venues to bring teams together to collaborate or simply to have fun.

The days of the dreaded commute to sit on our laptops for eight-plus hours at a desk were well and truly over. Swapped instead with the excitement of a rarer day catching up with colleagues.

The reality was that lockdowns and our new worlds also called out that the world had become a very lonely place for many during and after the pandemic; the transformation of our lives, the changes to how we work and, in turn, lived really was unprecedented. While we quietly 'got on with it', the need for a place to work and interaction along with the introduction of Digital Assistants such as Scout gave us far more.

On the good days, Scout is my assistant. On the bad days, she is my companion. To millions of isolated people throughout the world, Scout became far more.

Resistance to Change

While the transformation felt very natural and obvious to many, not everyone felt the same way. The news headlines in the early stages of the pandemic were filled with industry leaders initially demanding the return of the workforce and their desire to restore the old ways of working – mainly driven by productivity concerns or in a bid to retain a culture of collaboration in their offices.

Opinions varied, and many did soften their stances and attitudes over time, either because of union interventions, an exodus of talent, or as a happy middle-ground – as noted earlier, the office was still important to many.

The reality was that lockdowns went on just a little too long, to the point of no return for many. We managed and, in many cases, prospered. We found a balance that worked for everyone and formed the new normal of work that was simply irreversible.

Resistance to these changing times wasn't just a leadership concern around productivity. Progressions in technology also saw many employees raise concerns that advances in Robotics and AI may impact, or already *had* impacted, their role as our newsreels were filled with stories of protests and industrial action as employees took to the streets to demand intervention and regulation in bold bids to save their jobs.

Both parties needed to understand that there was not only a need to constantly evolve but, in turn, to also improve our skills with technology.

the story of scout

Change was certain and frequent, and while technology grew exponentially and societal transformation was more linear, and the two should happen in lockstep, progress didn't have the manners to wait for us to catch up, which caught many people out.

This resistance to change, coupled with a lack of training, led to a massive skill shortage and, in turn, a battle for talent from employers.

Old headlines concerned that employing teams of Robots would make us redundant only showed one side of the coin. The reality was that, yep, sure, the Robots came and displaced some workers in certain functions, but these bots and machines needed programming, repairing, servicing, updating, and CoBotic operators.

The Robotics and AI industry grew to the point that it created far more jobs than it initially displaced.

Many Governments struggled to see the introductions and disruptions on the horizon, challenged further by a lack of appreciation for the pace of change underway, and individuals were left to up-skill and retrain themselves in order to stay relevant.

In hindsight, and with some frustration for many, much of this disruption was preventable. This was not the first time in history that machines and technology had displaced workforces. The introduction of machines in the mills of the 1800s and the automation of production lines in the mid to late 1900s being just two examples of the impact of new technologies on lives and the significant societal transformation this can lead to.

There was also a lack of skilled labour entering the workforce. As brilliant as our education systems were, teachers were frustrated that the curriculums were not moving in line with the progressions of technology, meaning many people left education equipped with the skills Robots were already taking over.

We split into two camps: those who could see the step change in play and the promise of opportunity, a group known as the Vital Few, and those who couldn't change, either daunted by the level of pace or complexity or simply holding on to familiar ways steadfastly.

I criticise no one in their attitude to the journey of change towards the Future Of Us.

While history tells us the lessons of the past, it certainly didn't come with an instruction book; everyone reacted in the way they felt was best for them at the time. For me personally, change was the only option as pretty much every part of my life, especially workwise, was rapidly digitised. And while I'm no spring chicken, I wasn't quite ready to hang up my hat and retire just yet.

Learning to stay relevant was the only option I had.

Those who could adapt and take action to up-skill became pretty hot property in the future. People used the time freed up by working less to learn more. And while we didn't all become computer Scientists, we stayed interested and curious and, in turn, relevant.

Hence, this is the reason I set Scout to actively seek suitable training courses and news of developments relevant to me and my job.

Despite various concerns of the interested parties – from individuals to organisations – overall, we found a great balance. Governments eventually caught up and became supportive both financially and progressively by introducing policies and regulations to both protect incomes and the critical evolution of skill.

People worked together, particularly those Vital Few and earlier adopters, who by supporting others eventually, collectively became the Vital Many.

The Human Factor

We stay(ed) relevant, not only because we embraced change by taking on new learning and prioritising our development, but also as we brought something Robots never could... the 'human factor'.

Improving our knowledge and having an overall increased awareness was considered as important as possessing technical skills. It was important to have empathy to understand emotion and react accordingly, the creativity to build amazing solutions and explore new ideas, or the leadership and motivation to build a culture people wanted to be part of.

AI is smart, sure. I wouldn't want to take one on in a game of chess. But seeing teams of people from across businesses ideate, solve problems, collaborate, and dream up new ideas is a future-proof skill set. As humans, we're pretty special. We perhaps just don't always appreciate it as we were initially so frequently compared to the machines.

Furthermore, human relevance actually grew.

It became less about sitting behind a desk and sending emails for eight hours a day and more about how we could use our increased instincts and creativity to add a human touch and provide better services and solutions for our customers. The human factor became the human differentiator.

As customers ourselves, we were all now very aware of the power of technology, and we all expected more from our suppliers and favoured brands when it came to interactions and customer service.

We wanted it all: fast self-serve options, a range of platforms to get stuff done, and the fallback of 'let me talk to someone'.

And while things improved to a point where that last option wasn't often needed, it became a differentiating factor for many businesses.

The education system evolved over time to better equip the workforce of tomorrow and to retrain the workforce of today; people took personal ownership for their ongoing educations and evolution of skills.

We will work for several different companies in the future for two reasons.

Firstly, the skills shortages became such a challenge that companies realised that sharing talent was a more viable option than fighting for it.

Secondly, we had more time because of AI, making us super-efficient, and not everyone wanted to work full-time.

The nine to five pattern was introduced in the early 1900s as a way to improve conditions for workers and to manage outputs; however, over the last hundred years, we'd grown pretty used to it.

Many in the future use the opportunity to work twice as efficiently and do the same work for two companies that they previously did for one and enjoy more 'me time' back as a result.

• • •

Future of the Home

As work is no longer the main focus of my day, I get to spend more time on my hobbies and interests, with far more focus on keeping fit and healthy.

Our homes evolved in the future as well, both as a result of our new ways of working and our improved work-life balance. Our homes also began to include a multitude of devices, speakers, comfy spots, booths, and, of course, white walls that allowed every wall to become a screen using AR.

After working with Scout, it's now over to the human factor as I join a number of calls to talk through my live projects and tasks.

Holding my gaze on the 'join meeting' icon, I begin to see the head-and-shoulder 3D hologram images of my colleagues appear.

Using my hand, I can grab and move their locations on my Halo. With three of them on this call, I choose to align them equally, side-by-side, in the centre of the screen, leaving space above them where we will share screens and content as part of our discussion. Two have joined as themselves, with the third as an avatar with a sign below them indicating that they are travelling.

We exchange our hellos and the usual chat about the weather and weekend plans as the screen-share then comes into view. We then get into the details of our current project.

This same technology is also used to speak to family and friends, with us choosing the room or location we are in. The technology is so advanced, the vision so clear, and the connectivity so fast that I can read expressions on faces and body language instantly.

Meetings and catch-ups done, Scout then reappears as we wrap up the work tasks, agreeing that she will keep me posted on updates throughout the day, allowing us to quickly check in and maintain progress. While we work far fewer hours, the hours themselves and the very nature of work is an ongoing process, albeit a very light-touch affair.

So, with work done, it's now time to take care of some domestic duties around the place, with a little help, of course, from my digital companion.

We are more than happy to pay for devices and solutions that improve our lives and housework, and domestic duties have always been an area of focus for technology providers. This stands true from the introduction of the washing machine back in the day to robot vacuum cleaners and digital fridges. If they can simplify our lives or give us time back, we'll buy them.

Scout acts as a conductor of an army of Robotic Devices, from drone dusters and robotic vacuum cleaners to floor moppers and ironing machines; there is very little for us to do by hand. Scout herself is also available as a physical Robot, but I prefer the portability of the virtual version that can travel with me throughout the day, and anywhere I go.

The fridge talks to the shopping applications, and we see summaries on digital notice boards in our kitchen, acting as reminders and allowing us to instantly add an item just by saying it while standing in front of it (these are advanced presence systems that know when we are looking at the shopping list). These notice boards can also show information instantly by voice, e.g., by saying 'show family calendar'.

Scout moves around with me throughout the day, either on a speaker in the room I'm currently in, on my Halo device, intelligently and instantly linking to the nearest TV screen/monitor, or on my mobile devices, ear pods, or watch, using my watch to keep me up-to-speed on anything urgent while in Do Not Disturb mode.

"*Ant, your ride is on its way and will be with you in five minutes.*"

With advances in technology, we don't need to leave the house for the majority of work-related roles. And, as we work less, we now use that time to socialise and, you guessed it, shop!

Socialising, shopping, and investing in our hobbies and interests will become big business in the future.

Goods are delivered 24/7 by a huge network of drones and autonomous electric vehicles that buzz around the skies and streets, constantly dropping off and collecting parcels and packages.

Our homes all have secure parcel drop-off points that look like our dustbins and include a range of locks and sensors, so we know what's arrived, as well as a rechargeable cold store to keep goods fresh. The days of launching a parcel over a garden gate or leaving it with your neighbour are a thing of the past.

"*Ant, your ride has arrived.*"

As I jump in the cab, the absence of a driver no longer concerns me like it used to.

After years of accident-free driverless riding, I'm now confident the technology in the car is actually safer and more reliable than we humans ever were. Robots don't need to look down at their phone to change the track on their music app or reply to a message.

Governments took a long time to pass the regulation on driverless cars, and with very good reason, but as technology progressed, the evidence of hard data was too strong to ignore; machines were far safer than humans when it came to driving cars.

It's a short journey, as the store is only fifteen minutes away. In fact, everything in the digital world is only fifteen minutes away in the future as part of both the government's carbon agenda and the efforts to rebuild economies after Covid.

Thousands of small, vibrant business communities were encouraged and supported by governments following Covid, and the removal of cash, a complete overhaul of the business tax system, and new data sharing applications resulted in small local businesses and Entrepreneurs thriving.

These more local amenities and services provided us with an almost old-fashioned, local community and village feel.

The tech giants still exist and play a very important role, but new government policies and interventions mean there is a greater balance compared to the previous digital dominance of a limited few – there's a focus on both collaboration and well-being to promote Digital Inclusion and prevent social isolation. Communities became communities once again thanks to digital interventions and allowed more people to play an active role.

As I sit back in the cab, Scout's voice returns.

"Some new notifications just received, Ant."

I'm now wearing my regular, glasses version of Halo, and if I prefer, I can choose to use the large screen built into the cab.

Scout appears in mid-air with the notifications pulsing around her on the screen. A friend has messaged and asked if I fancy a trip to the gym. Scout and my friend's digital assistant have, in seconds, checked our schedules to find out if it's possible or not, and may ask if we wish to move things around to make it fit if not.

In the past, work occupied so much of our time we missed out on many social interactions such as this. But now, my settings are set to prioritise social interaction and healthy activity.

"That's great, Scout. Tell him I look forward to seeing him there."

We arrive at the store, and an icon appears in the top-left screen of my glasses as I enter, indicating they are an AR-enabled store. Then, a quick tap on the arm of my glasses will open the interactive applications they have available.

I could have chosen to pick up a Halo headset at the door, similar to the one I use at home – but these look more like the Perspex Covid face-visors people used during the pandemic. Stores provide these for all customers as an option, aware that not everyone has or uses AR Glass yet. You simply pick it up on your way into the store and leave it in a drop zone as you leave.

Retail locations of the future are very different places; they are made up of some key big players but also hundreds of local suppliers and small businesses in line with new inclusive government policies.

The spreading of wealth and employment is a top priority in the future, and while corporate dominance and reach are still present in some areas, it is quickly addressed, as the balance is required to ensure and maintain a more circular and stable future economy.

Covid changed the landscape of many industries, and the global economy forced governments to intervene to balance not just wealth but also the business models of many organisations (both large and small) in order to survive and maintain essential services and wider employment.

I pause as a message flashes up in the top right-hand corner of my glasses.

This time, it's an offer on something in the store that I might be interested in. Holding my gaze or saying 'open now' brings up more detail, and as I look at the item on the shelf, I begin to see and hear more information as a mini fanfare of information about the item appears on my Glass.

Future of Retail

Aside from the novelty of this new interactive digital and physical shopping experience, the future saw the introduction of many new data-sharing retail, marketing, and experience applications. Applications that collated information on what we were in the market to buy or were interested in, but which didn't need us to share heaps of our data with retailers or service providers until we were ready.

So here, as I walk around the stores, my shopping wish list is available for all to see, but while I see their offers and promotions, they don't see my personal data.

They simply know that I'm in the market for, say a birthday present for my son, that he is 12 years old, likes gaming, and I have a budget in mind of what I want to spend.

They don't know who I am personally as only the required data to provide a possible match is sent to them via an application, which they sign up to in advance. So now as I walk around the store or the shopping mall, I'm happy to have offers fired at me via my Glass telling me more about what they can offer.

I'm shopping, after all; this shouldn't be a guessing game, I'm in need of inspiration sometimes, and the future certainly provides plenty of that.

When I see an appropriate offer, I say "buy" and then simply walk away and continue shopping with the item already on its way to my home via the delivery network I mentioned earlier. We call this 'follow me home', but it's usually already there before me using out-of-town distribution locations to hold the goods.

This changed the future of marketing forever, and shopping became far more interesting as content and promotions became far more relevant and engaging.

Marketers used this always-on opportunity to the max, and we love it. Everyone in-store sees things of interest to them, and virtual digital displays above each store present a slightly different personalised image based on who's looking.

Many mourned the death of the high street following the growth and convenience of online, but our beloved high street and cities didn't die as many expected. Instead, they evolved and became far more interactive. We love to shop, and this doesn't change in the future.

It's now just digitally enhanced.

Scout gets in on the action as well, fully aware of everything I see and also working behind the scenes using the data sets in the wider shopping mall to great effect.

"*Ant, you must head toward the X store, they have something pretty special they would like you to see, and it sounds a good match.*"

With work completed in the morning, digital retail therapy out of the way, and a gym session completed while catching up with my old friend, life in the modern digital world feels very different to the long working hours and rushed social lives of the past.

Societal transformation was and still is the greatest driver of real change, and long may it continue in the Future Of Us.

The Digital Disconnect

The family are now all home from jobs, shopping, and schools and we share stories of our days. As we do this, we ask Scout to 'Cloak' us. This sees all Digital Services placed on pause with no notifications and no alerts; we are officially all off-grid. This is an essential tech sabbatical allowing us to be a family without digital interruptions.

The 'Cloak' is not just a digital disconnect. It's also a critical security and digital management tool. Cyber security has become one of the biggest challenges in the Future Of Us because as technology evolved, so too did the threats.

Cyber security has become one of the biggest industries in the world, with governments across the globe considering the threat of a cyber-attack more damaging than that of physical conflict.

Everyone has a Cloak, which is linked to biometric security by using our eyes and voices as a form of unique authentication – voice and retina passwords are the only things hackers can't replicate.

The Cloak also links our family's digital worlds together. It keeps our kids safe online, constantly reviewing their interactions and privacy online. It avoids a Big Brother reality by allowing Scout to monitor activity and possible threats and to take action as required in an isolated space, reporting to us only if necessary.

Scout is linked to other Cloaks across the globe as part of a global child safety policy that every government signed up to.

A common challenge across many Digital Solutions and services was that undesirables were more advanced and digitally adept than the likes of you and me. We lost control and awareness of the risk and dangers of the digital world here and there, but with lessons learnt the hard way, we came together and demanded that we all make the safety of children online our highest priority.

This sees Cloaks sharing information on potential breaches and risks and allows the self-learning systems to step up protection as required.

The Cloak also acts as a family agent for agreeing and managing screen time for our children.

Pre-agreed family policies are put into place and managed by Scout and the family's AI assistants, who then act as the digital parent and are given that dreaded task of bringing screen time to an end.

The policy allows a healthy balance of screen time and time away, with a wide range of available templates featuring 'good' policies recommended when we install our digital shields on children's devices, which evolve with the child as they grow, constantly encouraging healthy habits and a good balance between on- and off-line time.

Beyond security and managing screen times, digital technologies had played an important role in keeping our children connected during the lockdowns to both their friends and their educations and while it felt like a novelty for many of us, the transition for them was very natural and obvious, as many children questioned why they ever needed to go back to a physical school again. And as parents managed their protests, what wasn't immediately obvious at the time was that this period had lit the touchpaper of a period of wider societal transformation that no one could have ever foreseen.

Over the years that followed our streets and parks fell eerily empty, as our young people now almost institutionalised to their digital interactions shied away from physical social situations and sadly grew more sedentary and physically disconnected due to the ease and convenience of their online worlds. In their eyes, they were more socially connected online and there simply was less need to go outside, as their richer online worlds gave them a far more convenient alternative with their preferred option of selective anonymity.

This transformation spread to the workforce of the future who gradually began to inherit them, along with their preference of working more online over physically connecting, starting a pattern and trend that would go on to transform the future of work forever.

We took Scout's recommendations for dinner, enjoyed an amazing meal, and added our own feedback and rating to the restaurant as the cab drops us off back home.

We thank our babysitter as she invoices us automatically upon leaving the house, her phone generating the bill on pre-agreed rates and acting as the time stamp; Scout settles it instantly.

"Welcome home, hope the restaurant was a hit, guys. I've done the kids' homework with them, and both piano lessons are completed. Both are doing really great and want to play what they've learnt so far to you tomorrow, so brace yourselves – we're still on level one, remember!"

The piano lessons and homework functions that Scout provides are just two examples of the many additional optional packages we can purchase, adding to what appears to be a sea of digital fees in the Future Of Us.

• • •

Life As A Service

The growing number of digital applications forming our Life As A Service collectively kick-started one of the biggest societal transformation in history, evolving the financial and economic landscape of many generations that followed.

We didn't realise it at the time, but this gradual increase in Things and Life 'As A Service' had started one of the biggest societal and economic shifts in history.

While gradual in its transformation, the wakening reality and effects of this evolution were felt far and wide and sadly too late for many.

For younger workers, there was the struggle to get onto the housing ladder, as their lower and often inconsistent incomes didn't cater for both their instant digital lives and the banks' tougher rules on affordability and required deposits to join the housing ladder.

The mid-tenure workforce, whose lives were growing increasingly more expensive, were exasperated by the increased cost of their children's lives as well, while pensions and investments not built for such change pushed the option of retirement plans further out for many of us.

The Life As A Service model continued to evolve and took opportunity, as we saw a growing number of Property As A Service models, almost providing a middle-ground service between a hotel and a rental property – everything from the furniture to the meals delivered was provided 'As A Service'.

This model became very popular with younger people who struggled to afford property. However, it came at a price, of course, often locking into convenience and ease.

The financial institutions, aware the digital industry was taking food from their table, adapted their models in response.

They provided longer-term and family mortgages with a far more flexible approach to lending overall. With changing attitudes to work and the growth of the Gig Economy, skills were in demand, but incomes were not always regular. The banks had to adapt out of necessity to suit a changing marketplace and customer.

The answer for many was to simply work longer, and as AI supported many roles, semi-retirement became a popular choice for many.

Many people chose the hours and roles they did, and this proved a win-win for the economy as it allowed organisations to hang on to critical skills and knowledge workers longer.

Sure, we will work less in the future. But we can work far longer and on our terms. Many had to.

However, while the majority of us had the means and skills to adapt, how did we address the growing Digital Divide and Digital Inclusion across society?

How did we ensure that everyone had the required access to Digital Services needed in their daily lives, and how did we ensure all children, regardless of circumstances, had adequate and equal opportunities in a digital world?

Everything from the devices, connectivity, and solutions needed to access education, entertainment, and social interactions all come at a digital price. Providing access to these systems resulted in the launch of a new government service called UDA (Universal Digital Access).

This was similar in design to the UBI (Universal Basic Income) systems that many countries had tried or were running in niche projects already. But unlike UBI, UDA only provided funds to cover the range of Digital Services needed to be present in our new digital worlds,

It was designed to ensure a level playing field for everyone; regardless of means or current situation, the services remained free to those in need, while they needed them.

It wasn't just a free-for-all; those who could afford it contributed towards or paid for services in full as part of their income tax returns, ensuring everyone had access and connectivity to their ever-growing digital lives.

The question of 'who foots the bill' for this quickly hit the tax-payer's agenda but was quickly addressed as awareness about the reality of who was profiteering from these increasing digital costs in our lives grew and governments introduced a step change in digital tax.

This tax meant those benefiting from the digital costs were then supporting digital access where appropriate.

Back to our evening. With our children soundly asleep and our feet up in front of the TV, it's now time to catch up on our favourite shows. We either project a show onto the wall in the room or place our individual Halos on if we are watching different shows, each using the same wall to project to but only seeing our chosen show or series.

We opt for individual programmes, and with Halo, on I choose to 'resume last watched'. The screen instantly resumes playing a film I started watching recently.

My mobile device also now springs to life as it offers me snippets of information and trivia on the film I'm watching.

Almost all media is now presented on two devices, the screen you're watching it on and then also your mobile device or glass. Due to the rising popularity of gaming over the years, the games industry overtook the film and TV industry many years ago, and they responded by making TV and film a far more interactive experience.

Many programmes now offer interactive viewer inputs, resulting in multiple different endings and taking you from passive viewer to interactor and building a far more involving experience.

Virtual Reality progressed from novelty solutions to become big in entertainment as well by offering us complete immersion into a scene, allowing us to choose our viewpoint, camera angle, or perspective from a character's vision.

Relaxed and refreshed from our days, we head to bed as Scout provides a brief summary of the next day, pushing reminders to appear on the bathroom mirror as I brush my teeth.

We sink into our Smart Bed that has already reached the perfect temperature and adjusted the firmness ahead of us getting in.

I now hear the familiar and final update of the day.

"House is now in night mode, all security services active and the family Cloak in place."

It may appear slightly strange that I talk to Scout so personally, as I thank her, rather than treating her like the machine she is.

The reality is that AI has advanced to such a point that services now include humour, emotion, and empathy as optional extras. Scout can pick up on my tone of voice and general mood as we communicate throughout the day and then adapts her interactions to support the bad days and make the very best of the good.

While AI may never understand true emotion, it can do some basic analysis, detect when things aren't quite right from a well-being perspective, then deploy a range of support services to help.

The overall progress of AI advances at such a pace in the future that almost every service and solution has AI at its core.

The growing world of connectivity in our lives brings what many would suggest as no more than the subjects of a Sci-Fi storyline. Yet the very real reality is it will bring change to our lives in ways I've covered here and many other ways in the future that we can't yet conceive.

Scout becomes more real every day. While I can't consider how I ever lived without her, I also knowingly ignore the reality that the relationship is one-way as I see the growing digital direct debits leave my account each month.

As services improve and are enhanced across my digital life, I try to consider, with a shiver, what would happen if I stopped paying them as more and more of my life becomes a Life As A Service experience.

Life's changed a lot in recent years; technology progressed rapidly and the pandemic has given us a chance to take stock and see different ways to live and work.

This change in wider societal preferences was instantly noticed by the big tech players, whose data showed the changing patterns and trends in play. And who, along with Innovators and Entrepreneurs, quickly delivered new services and exciting solutions to both support our daily lives and capture our digital spend.

The acceleration continued as we lived through the most significant and impactful phase of the Industrial and Digital revolutions. Overall, we've come a long way. But evidence and opinions suggest we ain't seen nothing yet... in the Future Of Us!

The walls of my room fill with a gradually fading image of a star-filled moonlight sky.

"*Goodnight, Ant.*"
"*Goodnight, Scout.*"

*'We've come a long way so far,
but we ain't seen nothing yet!'*

1
introduction

'The best way to predict the future is to create it.'
Abraham Lincoln

Introduction

So, will the Story of Scout ever be realised?
Will these Artificial Intelligence solutions soon begin to appear in our lives?
And what might we have missed in taking this glance towards the future?
Or are these ideas and concepts simply the visions of a creative imagination and safer for the storylines of a Sci-Fi movie?
Well, the interesting point is that all the technologies I described already exist!
To make the Story of Scout a reality needs no invention, only innovation to bring these solutions to life, as a service.
Everything from the hardware to the software is already available in some shape or form. However, while some are slightly more basic than I describe here, others are actually far more advanced as progressions in AI and Quantum Computing hold the promise of some truly incredible features that will have a significant impact on our lives in the future.
All that is needed is the innovation and creativity of Innovators, Entrepreneurs, and tech giants. These are the people who will have those light bulb ideas and then will develop these into solutions and the next big thing that we simply can't live without.
With progress driven by the constant advent of new technologies and the exponential pace of change underway coupled with changing societal attitudes to the way we live and work, we are likely to see more progress and transformation over our lifetimes than at any other stage in history.
We will become the topic of future history lessons as children are told of how a pandemic started one of the most significant societal evolutions of all time and how technology aided the transformation of our lives forever.
And forgive me for not painting a more futuristic story of Scout, with wild inventions and predictions of Sci-Fi devices and solutions completely transforming life as we know it. But the purpose of this book is not to predict the technologies of the future but instead to help us navigate

and adapt to the technologies that are already here and already transforming our lives.

Some incredible developments in technology have already transformed the way we live and work today, and the current pace and progression of technology underway are likely to bring further transformations to our lives.

We may struggle to comprehend this change today, but in time, it will become our 'new normal' in the Future Of Us.

About Me

I've worked in the digital industry for close to thirty years, witnessing, during this time, some considerable technology transformations and societal evolutions. From the growth of the Internet, the mass adoption of mobile devices, and the roll-out of the data networks that connect everything and everyone to the birth of social media.

I work for a global digital communication organisation, where I head up the innovation, engineering and managing architect teams

I work with an awesome team, a truly inspiring leader and some amazing customers, where together, we research, ideate, test, and trial new technologies in a bid to explore their value, viability, and reality. I've supported some of the world's largest brands, providing thought leadership, subject matter expertise, and general guidance to support them in navigating both their own journeys and transformations, but most importantly, the development of their people and teams in how they stay informed and relevant today and tomorrow.

It was as part of my day job in 1999 that I had the privilege to meet Neil Armstrong and listen to the experiences of his incredible journey to the moon.

This was when I started to really consider the truly incredible feats of innovation and engineering that made his journey possible. And I also considered the question of where technology and innovation might take us in the future and our own journeys through the Digital Revolution.

Introduction

While we might struggle to compare with a moon landing, let's not limit our thinking. With controversial innovators such as Elon Musk in our midst and the fact that we all hold devices in our pockets with 100,000 times more computing power than it took to put a man on the moon, who knows what might be possible today and where innovation might take us tomorrow?

What We'll Cover

So, as the line between traditional and digital technologies blurs, we begin to see our lives, roles, and organisations transform into more, either driven by new technologies, competitive marketplaces and customer expectations, or indeed our own changing attitudes towards work, our purpose, and who we work for.

Overall, we are on the cusp of significant change but without a crystal ball or map to show us the way.

Our lives over the next ten to twenty years will be the topic of future history lessons as teachers explain our lives of today to children who would struggle to comprehend our current reality.

Over the course of this book, we're going to look at the changes and transformations of the past and the trends and patterns of the evolutions currently underway as we consider our own development and approaches in our own bids to stay relevant and informed for the future.

We'll explore:
Our Time in History
We'll take a look back over history at previous stages of the Industrial Revolution. We'll explore how previous innovations impacted the way people lived and worked, asking what lessons we can learn from the outcomes of previous innovations and societal transformations.
The Drivers & Urgency
Here we'll look closer at our time in history. What are the likely innovations and drivers that will impact our lives

and careers? And why will our time be far faster and more impacting than those of previous generations?

Understanding It All

How can we better understand the often-confusing world of technology and the different components at play? After all, we're not technical, right? Sure. But technology aside, how do we understand, accept, and embrace change? Where should we spend our time, and how do we prepare for change?

The Key Impacts on Our Lives

While change is inevitable, and we can learn heaps from history, it's impossible to predict any precise changes. Though, whatever happens, progress will inevitably impact two key areas in our lives, how we earn and, in turn, how we spend money. So, in this chapter, we will look at the impact of innovation on the Future Of Work and the cost of our digital lives in a Life As A Service world.

Staying Relevant

As the world progresses at pace and we struggle to keep up with the constant advent of new innovations, technologies, and headlines filled with suggestions of how Robots and machines may take our jobs, how do we stay relevant and prepare for the inevitable change ahead?

We've Already Come a Long Way

As we begin to focus our thoughts on the Future Of Us, some may raise an eyebrow or smile in disbelief at some of my suggestions in the Story of Scout, and unfortunately, we don't have a crystal ball to know for sure what the future may hold.

However, while the Story of Scout may seem some time ahead of us, let's pause to consider some of the incredible innovation progressions of our Digital Revolution so far.

These are innovations that, while often subtle in their introductions and adoptions, have gone on to transform our lives, entire industries, and the fortunes of many.

Introduction

Picture the scene: we're at a dinner party fifteen years ago, and I told you...

That in the future, you will find it very difficult to leave the house without your smartphone. It holds everything from your wallet to your playlists, your emails, and social media feeds that you would struggle to go a day, if not hours, without seeing.

That we could speak to a virtual assistant to search the Internet, turn lights on and off, the heating up and down, order goods, play music, or settle an argument... all without touching your phone.

That we could order pretty much anything, and it would arrive the next day, if not the same day, and we would happily pay an annual subscription for the certainty.

That Uber would disrupt an entire industry pretty much overnight, allowing you to order a cab from anywhere without even knowing the address, and you would pay automatically without touching your wallet.

That a fast-food ordering application business would be valued at more than some of our leading supermarkets, all without owning a single pizza shop or takeaway... *did somebody say, Just Eat?*

That Airbnb would revolutionise the whole hotel industry and be valued at more than many hotel chains put together, all without owning a single mattress or trouser press, let alone a hotel.

That we would stop watching TV and renting movies but would instead stream shows for a monthly subscription.

That the last four or five examples are applications that a coder/developer could knock up a basic version of in just a few hours and launch for a couple of hundred pounds.

That an electric car would travel over 400 miles on a single charge and beat a Ferrari in a drag race.

That the same electric car maker would also send reusable rockets to space while eyeing up the colonisation of Mars.

I'm certain at this point you would have been looking for the door.

But there's more. What if I told you:

That it would be close to impossible to prise our children from their headsets and screens to go and play outside.

That we would use video calling applications to work from home and, in most cases, improve our efficiency in doing so.

That we would be able to home-school our children by beaming a teacher into our homes and continuing their education during the lockdowns.

That if you stopped paying your digital connectivity direct debits, you would lose access to all your photographs, all your music, all your social media feeds, and you would have to commute to the office every day for your nine to five to do your jobs.

Go back and read that last one again... makes us think, right? Subtle or not, these are just a few examples of how innovation has already transformed our lives.

So, back to that dinner party.

Whether you lean in with interest or raise an eyebrow while looking for the exit, know that the future holds little regard for our opinions anyway.

Innovators will keep innovating; disrupters will keep enhancing and disrupting our lives, and some of the highest-paid executives in industry completely missed the disruption of some of these new services that we now take for granted in our everyday lives.

The future is well underway and accelerating at pace.

The only choice we have is the journey we take and how we enjoy the ride. It's our time. It's our Future.

*'Lessons from our Past
become our guides for the Future.'*

2
our time in history

'Life can only be understood backwards, but it must be lived forward.'
Thomas Frey

the future of us

New technologies transforming the way people live and work is nothing new.

Consider the technology in our lives today: the car, train, and aeroplane; electricity and the television; computers, the Internet, and the mobile phone. These are all things that we perhaps take for granted in our lives today, but all of which played a major role in transforming the lives of the generations before us and shaping our modern society as we know it.

Imagine removing just one of these – how different would your life be?

Would your industry and job even exist?

How would your day differ?

And though we look back and talk of these innovations as history, modern man has been on earth for over 200,000 years. The majority of these innovations took place over the last 250 years of the Industrial Revolution. This means these all happened in 0.1% of man's time on earth, making this time really live up to its name of a true revolution.

Revolution.
Noun
- *a sudden, radical, or complete change.*

And while it seems rapid, it's taken many of these innovations time to really take hold.

Progress has been fairly linear and gradual overall, affording people time to transform and adjust. And other than the odd exception, many innovations needed other components to allow them to take off.

Home computers needed microchips, Electric cars needed better batteries, smartphones needed high-speed data networks, and social media needed 'us' to share our pictures and posts, all of which took time.

our time in history

Technology Growth Acceleration

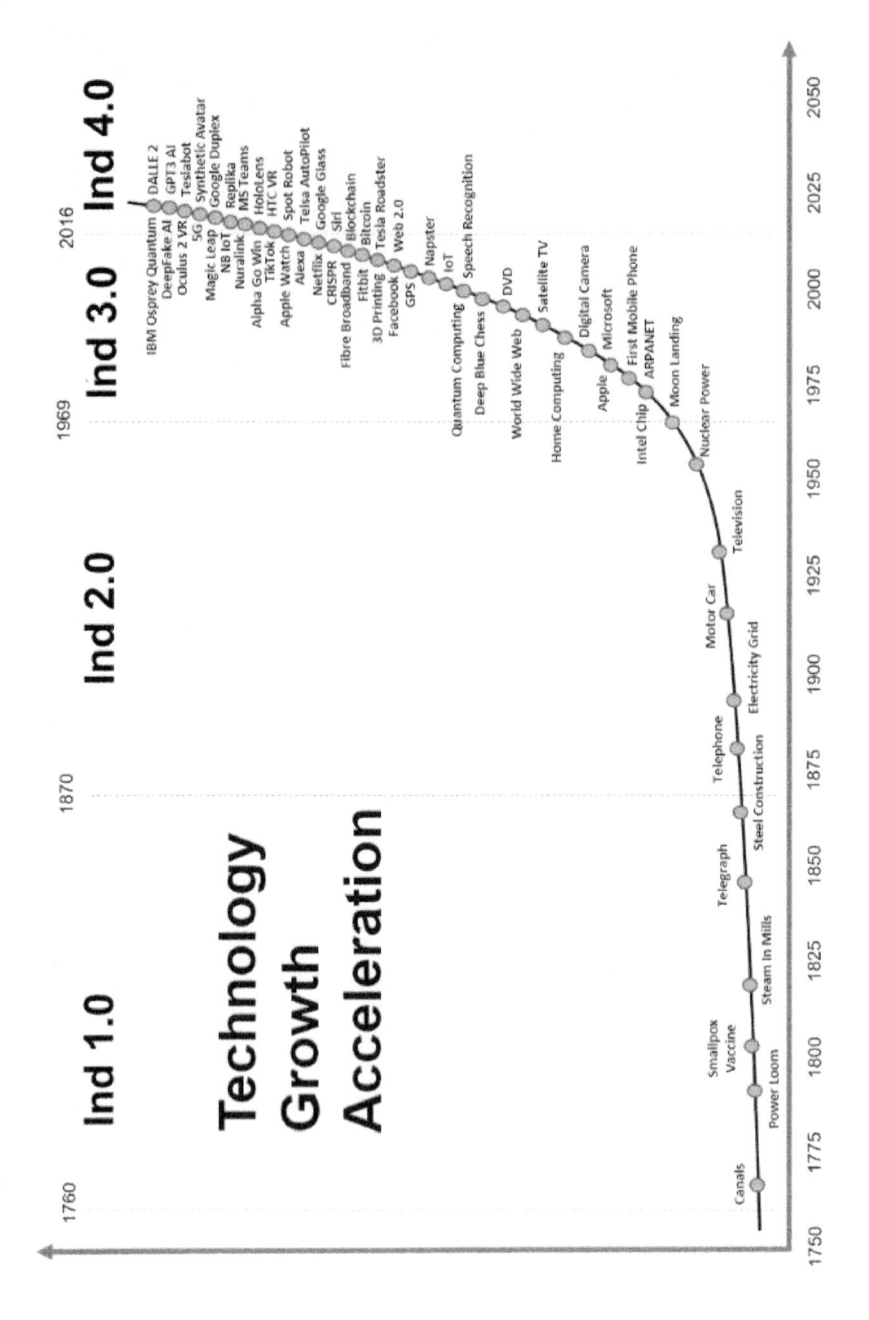

Ind 1.0 (1760) — Canals, Power Loom, Smallpox Vaccine, Steam In Mills

Ind 2.0 (1870) — Telegraph, Steel Construction, Telephone, Electricity Grid, Motor Car, Television

Ind 3.0 (1969) — Nuclear Power, Moon Landing, ARPANET, First Mobile Phone, Intel Chip, Apple, Microsoft, Digital Camera, Home Computing, Satellite TV, DVD, World Wide Web, Deep Blue Chess, Quantum Computing, Speech Recognition, GPS, IoT, Napster, Web 2.0, Facebook, 3D Printing, Fitbit, Fibre Broadband, Bitcoin, CRISPR, Netflix, Blockchain, Apple Watch, Siri, Alexa, TikTok, Google Glass, Alpha Go Win, Spot Robot, Nuralink, HTC VR, Tesla AutoPilot, NB IoT, MS Teams, Replika, Magic Leap, 5G, Google Duplex, Oculus 2 VR, Synthetic Avatar, Deepfake AI, Tesla Roadster, Tesibot

Ind 4.0 (2016) — IBM Osprey Quantum, DALLE 2, GPT3 AI

Timeline: 1750, 1775, 1800, 1825, 1850, 1875, 1900, 1925, 1950, 1975, 2000, 2025, 2050

All images are also available to view and download at **www.futureofus.co.uk**

But as we look to the later stages of the revolution so far, we see a steep progress curve that brings us to our present-day as the pace of new innovations accelerates exponentially.

With the data suggesting that history has a habit of repeating itself, it's safe to say that things are likely to develop even faster over the years ahead.

So, what can we learn from the history of innovation and if we look to the **Technology Growth Acceleration** graph over the wider Industrial Revolutions? We get that it's nothing new, and we are clearly not the first generations to live through times of significant transformation and change.

But how did previous innovations change the way people worked and, in turn, lived?

And what can we learn from this, as individuals, as we start to build our own plans for the future?

In business, we build strategies and plans for the future based on what we know and, where available, data, hard facts and evidence. Guessing is not a great strategy, so we focus on what we know from our experiences, we survey the markets, we test customer sentiment, and we hire experts.

Through change, we look for opportunities to do things differently, constantly striving to improve services to find unique selling points and differentiators that will give customers a compelling reason to choose us over competitors.

I propose we treat our career as a business and ourselves as evolving products. We should follow the same principles and approaches in our assessments of what we need to know and learn and how we should develop to stay relevant in the Future Of Us.

After all, we can't make decisions for our futures based on guesses, luck, or predictions alone. We need to look at hard facts, evidence, and data wherever possible.

So, in this chapter, I want to take a quick look at the key innovations delivered over various stages of both the Industrial Revolution and the current Digital Revolution. I will explore some of the technologies and societal evolutions, as well as the transformations they drove, keeping as brief as possible to avoid this turning into a history lesson. I will focus on limited but key innovations that have had a subsequent impact on our lives today.

As we walk through, ask yourself: What can we learn from the past?

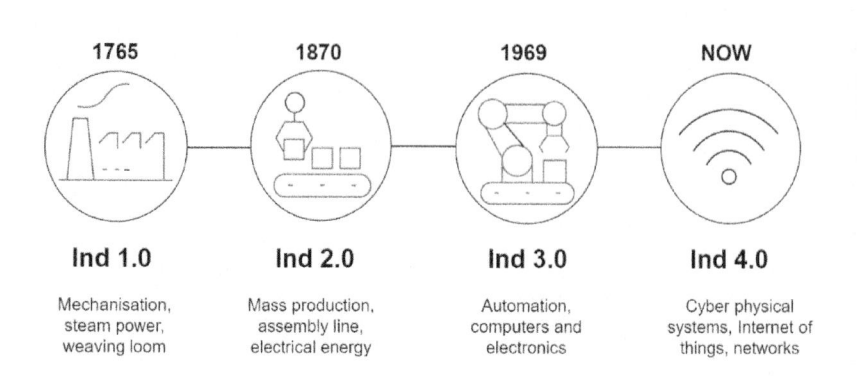

• • •

1765	1870	1969	NOW
Ind 1.0	**Ind 2.0**	**Ind 3.0**	**Ind 4.0**
Mechanisation, steam power, weaving loom	Mass production, assembly line, electrical energy	Automation, computers and electronics	Cyber physical systems, Internet of things, networks

Ind 1.0_ Mechanisation 1765–1870

Up until the mid-1700s, people mainly made their living through agriculture and handicrafts. A pattern that hadn't really changed for many hundreds, if not thousands, of years. The first Industrial Revolution delivered a number of key innovations and a pattern of urbanisation that individually and then collectively completely transformed the lives of many, paving the way for much of our modern society.

Key Innovations

- **1700:** The first factories and mills, powered by water and horsepower.

- **1761:** The Bridgewater Canal opens, connecting cities in the northwest of England. A purpose-built

the future of us

connection canal that proved to be very successful and highly profitable. This was the Internet of its time.

- **1778:** The power loom weaving process arrives as the first machines started to automate processes usually carried out by humans.

- **1798:** Edward Jenner develops the first vaccine for smallpox, the same vaccine structure that was used to tackle Covid.

- **1801:** The first electric battery was invented in the late 1700s but was mastered in 1801 by Alessandro Volta with the development of his voltaic pile, allowing the mass production of the world's first batteries.

- **1802:** The adoption of steam engines into mills and factories, providing a constant supply of power, allowing production to be 24/7.

- **1822:** Charles Babbage begins to build the first mechanical computer and is considered the father of computing.

- **1827:** Greg Ohm publishes his theory of Ohm's law, which is used to show the relationship between current, voltage, and resistance of electric circuits.

- **1834:** Moritz Von Jacobi invents the first practical electric motor. This goes on to drive an array of future innovations and play a key role in powering industries.

- **1838:** Samuel Morse introduces the Telegraph and Morse Code system, starting the communication network of the day and instantly making the world a smaller place as people communicated almost instantly over greater distances.

- **1845:** Portland cement transforms the construction industry.

our time in history

- **1855:** Sir Henry Bessemer develops a method of mass-producing steel that is quicker, less labour intensive, and far cheaper, driving transformation in both machine manufacturing and building process methods. This goes on to give birth to the high-rise buildings and skyscrapers of our city skylines.

→ **Societal Impacts**

Fitting its name, the first Industrial Revolution really was truly revolutionary in every way. In the mid-1700s, new manufacturing processes driven by the introduction of machines completely transformed the way people lived and worked.

By the early 1800s, automation improvements and the introduction of steam replaced water and manpower, providing a constant source of power and massively increasing production.

Automation, while increasing output, did also displace many jobs in the early stages of the revolution as machines delivered improved efficiency in the mill and factory processes.

People initially fought back, with the short-lived Luddite uprising using sabotage as a negotiation, supposedly smashing up machines in protest at machines taking their jobs.

The introduction of steam power did ultimately have the opposite effect. As the constant supply of power and further development of factory machines over time led to a massive increase in productivity, there was a huge increase in overall employment.

This resulted in a mass migration of the workforce from the countryside farms to work in the new and now sprawling factories of the growing smog-filled cities.

Production was endlessly driven solely by profit, and entire families worked around the clock to provide the labour needed to deliver incredible growth.

The cities were not designed for this steep increase in levels of occupancy, and this, coupled with increasing growth in population, resulted in some pretty horrible conditions for many.

Conditions were cramped, nutrition poor, and disease rife as cholera spread through factories, taking almost as many lives as the accidents – health and safety were prioritised far below profit.

People worked around the clock in twelve-hour shifts, and child exploitation was commonplace. Children as young as four years old were considered an essential part of the workforce, as their small size allowed them to work within the machines themselves.

Overall, life wasn't very satisfying for people in the early 1800s and with only a small percentage of society able to vote, people had no voice to stress the hardships they were enduring.

Some positive societal innovations did follow, however, such as the Factory Act of 1833 and Mines Act of 1842, which prohibited the employment of children under the age of nine and limited the hours children between nine and thirteen could work.

But however positive these steps were, it's still impossible to imagine this in comparison to our very comfortable lives today.

Further innovation did follow as some factory owners took steps to improve the quality of lives of the workforce. They did this either by operating with more humanitarian intentions or moving their factories out of the cities, building purpose-built factories and entire towns to house workers in far improved and more comfortable conditions in a bid to attract and retain the best workforce.

They provided work, accommodation, and decent food in return for unquestionable loyalty. And while still a form of exploitation, alternate conditions were incomparable, and people flocked to these new opportunities with their families.

Many of these factory owners went on to provide far more than work and shelter.

They provided education for both children and the workforce and encouraged their workers to open and extend their minds, as a benefit and in a bid to retain, educate, and upskill their workforce for the jobs of tomorrow.

These interventions and actions resulted in the landscape we see today, making up many of our towns and cities. And while the mills and pits closed long ago, the houses and communities still exist.

→ Learning & Observations

Conditions were so stark in comparison to our modern lives that it can feel very difficult to compare the two or to really learn from the past. However, there are surprisingly many key lessons we can take.

Despite often being purely driven by profit, mill and factory owners of the first Industrial Revolution were the innovators of their time. Their introduction of machines to improve efficiency and drive profits started a transformation never seen before, even though the idea of machines taking humans' jobs feels very much like a headline of today.

The term 'Luddite' remains with us to this day as we see pockets of resistance to change in our own organisations and families, and innovations quickly progress with little regard to our views and opinions.

Many people and organisations will take lessons from the past, but as a plethora of much-loved brands disappear from our world, we know not everyone will see or embrace change. They will resist it to futile ends.

We can't really compare with the unsatisfying lives of the workforce of this time, but capitalism's profit-first approach is perhaps a sobering reminder of the purpose of our shareholder or investor-owned businesses.

We should all consider our purpose as organisations and individuals as the modern workforce now places a higher weight on the purpose of the organisations they work with and for.

The bid to improve the lives of the workforce through better conditions and education also sounds familiar.

Today, organisations also look at how they can become better and more attractive employers to the modern workforce, with a focus on work-life balance and well-being high on every organisation's agenda. They wish to ensure they are best placed to invest and up-skill their workforces for new technologies or out of necessity to attract talent.

While innovation initially migrated the workforce to the cities, this trend of moving people away again lends to a trend similar to our current time.

As innovative, flexible working solutions allowed people to work from home during the Covid pandemic, leaving us to question the role of the office, the nine to five structure, and our need to live in or near cities.

This stage of societal transformation is still underway as we see our regional economies grow in response to our needs and the looming question of how the new normal might look.

Maybe this initially almost incomparable time period actually does have a number of similarities and lessons after all.

Ind 2.0_ Mass Production & Electrification 1870–1969

The introduction of electricity, gas, and oil as replacements for steam power rapidly transformed almost every industry again.
    This provided more manageable and accessible power sources to aid a wide range of processes and progressive automation, which in turn greatly increased the mass production of consumer goods.
    This period also witnessed a broad number of significant innovations, such as the motor car, the telephone, the typewriter, and a range of scientific

discoveries, making it fitting for its name: the Technological Revolution.

Key Innovations

- **1874:** The introduction of the QWERTY keyboard typewriter starts, for many of us, a skill we just kinda learned over time.

- **1876:** Alexander Graham Bell move us from Morse Code and Telegraphs to the transmission of voice via the telephone and possibly one of the most important and significant inventions of our time.

- **1879:** Joseph Swan and Thomas Edison both patent a functional light bulb.

- **1882:** Thomas Edison switched on the first grid powered by electricity which becomes the model for the modern power grids of today and completely transforms lives.

- **1886:** Carl Gassner invents the first dry cell battery enabling portable power across a number of devices, from radios to lighting, the innovations of their day.

- **1886:** Karl Benz invents the first petrol or the gasoline-powered motor car.

- **1892:** John Froelich introduces the tractor, taking innovation back to the countryside and greatly increasing agricultural productivity; this starts a transformation of food production at scale.

- **1895:** Guglielmo Marconi invents a system of wireless communications using radio waves. This is the early concept of what is now, in reality, our mobile phone networks of today.

- **1899:** Waldemar Lungner invents a range of batteries that go on to improve the portable electronic device sector.

- **1902:** Edgar Purcell patents the Tarmac process, previously invented by John McAdams in the early 1800s, which allows rapid construction of the highway networks that played a critical role in the transportation of goods and business travel for many generations that followed. The growth of the highway networks is the high-speed Internet of its time.

- **1926:** Henry Ford begins mass production of his Model T, bringing affordable motoring to the masses and putting the world on wheels.

- **1926:** John Logie Baird demonstrates the world's first live working television system.

- **1932:** Frank Whittle is granted a patent for his design of a turbojet engine that would go on to power the world of air travel.

- **1938:** Chemists Otto Hahn and Fritz Strassmann and physicists Lise Meitner and Otto Robert Frisch discover Nuclear Fission, leading to nuclear power, but their research also goes on to influence the Soviet atomic bomb project.

- **1951:** Nuclear power is used to produce power for households for the first time.

- **1954:** George Devol invents the first digitally operated, programmable Robot called Unimate, which lays the foundations for the modern Robotics Industry.

- **1956:** The hard disk is invented by IBM.

- **1957:** IBM launch the first personal computer controlled by a keyboard.

- **1960s:** Wide deployment of Robots in production lines, mainly comprising hydraulic and pneumatics for heavy lifting or high-speed repetitive processes.
- **1961:** The first crewed spaceflight achieved by Vostok 1.
- **1969:** ARPANET becomes the first wide area packet network, using the technologies that go on to form the technical foundations for what is the Internet of today.
- **1969:** Apollo 11 takes Neil Armstrong, Buzz Aldrin, and Michael Collins to the moon, marking a fitting end to this period of incredible progress.

→ **Societal Impacts**

The wealth divide grew in the early stages of the Industrial Revolution. You either owned a mill or factory, or you worked in one.

Thankfully, working conditions continued to improve through the Second Revolution, driven either by new regulations, in bids to attract talent, or to retain skilled employees.

The introduction of the internal combustion engine kick-started the motor industry in 1876. It would go on to be the driving force (excuse the pun) for growth across many other industries as a quicker and far more flexible means of transportation for goods and people.

Henry Ford embraced this innovation, and using mass production, he transformed the lives of many.

He brought affordable motoring to the masses with the launch of the Ford Model T in 1908. However, it was his next innovation in 1926 that would bring possibly the most significant social transformation of all time – and it's completely unrelated to technology.

In 1926 Henry Ford embraced the American Labor Union's nine to five idea and introduced this into his factories, moving people from gruelling six-day, twelve-hour shifts of seventy-two hours a week to forty hours over five days, measuring output rather than time worked.

This introduced the pattern of work we are familiar with today. He also took this a step further and, in a bold step forward, increased the wages of his workforce.

His actions were met with utter outrage and challenge from business and industry leaders at the time. Many called him reckless and foolish as they protested to the government in a bid to prevent him from setting this new pattern of work and higher salaries.

Their efforts were in vain, and Ford's new proposals were actively supported by the government and went on to form the basis of the Fair Labor Standards Act (FLSA) of 1938, which curbed the exploitation of factory workers.

Ford's logic was clear and brought positive change to the lives of many, but it was not without purposeful intention and personal gain.

Capitalism and charity are not natural bed partners; history and the present day remind us of this.

Ford was mass producing a product that only a limited number of people in society could afford or had the lifestyle and free time to enjoy. His changes created a market for his product, using his own workforce as a lever, knowing full well that it would drive far wider adoption.

This quickly allowed him to build one of the most successful businesses and industries of all time. This market-creating move led to perhaps the most significant societal evolution ever, generating a global increase in consumers and, whether intentional or not, he inadvertently provided the basis of growth for many other industries and massively improved the quality of life for millions, now able to enjoy their weekends.

Governments backed these industry-led innovations, which were in lock step with the earlier introductions of minimum wage in 1909 and general elections in 1918, which gave the working-class workforce a far greater voice in matters pertaining to working conditions and their health and safety.

Also, in 1938, a law was introduced that allowed people to take paid holidays from work, known as the Summer

Holiday Revolution. In that same year, it was also prohibited to employ anyone under the age of 16 in manufacturing or mining.

In another bid to improve lives and protect workers, the welfare system was introduced in 1945 in the UK, with a focus on health, education, and employment protection providing support to workers and their families.

Labour unions grew, new regulations continued, and with greater voice and vastly improved working conditions, much-needed work-life balance was brought to society. This completely transformed people's lives and is a pattern we still follow to this day.

Another example of similar nontechnical innovation followed in 1933 when tyre manufacturer Michelin launched the Michelin guide, a motorist manual encouraging motorists to drive more and visit listed restaurants.

More frequent driving created a greater need for tyres and provided significant growth for Michelin. This move also started a theme of motoring for pleasure over purpose, and in time would see an innovation to not only drive more tyre sales but to be the highest achievement in culinary skill for chefs around the world.

The two World Wars brought unthinkable challenges to people's lives across many continents, with innovations in warfare and weaponry, tactics, and code helping bring the wars to an end.

The Space Race and Moon Landing then brought the promise of brighter days ahead.

Innovations that initially took people away from farms then returned people to them as mechanised farm equipment changed how food was produced, turning agriculture into a big industry.

The development of the rail networks, bicycle, and car made travel for work and pleasure far more accessible.

Baby Boomers of the Second World War hit the workforce at the end of this stage, bringing an army of labour and talent to industries and fuelling the growth of many. And, with a quality of life significantly better than their parents, the mass workforce led to greater growth.

This was a busy and significant period of transformation, delivering many of the current ways of modern life and working we are familiar with today.

→ **Learning & Observations**

Henry Ford's innovations were just that. He didn't really invent anything; he took a recent invention to the next stage using innovative methods of mass production and then created a market for the growth of his product.

It's hard to say which was the more important and if one could have been maintained without the other.

Innovation over invention was a strong theme at this stage of the Revolution. And, if we look to more recent times, innovations have followed a similar theme in examples such as Uber.

Uber didn't invent ride sharing, but in removing cash from the payment and tipping process and showing you the location and ETA of your ride, they addressed key problems with previous taxi systems and totally captured the market as a result.

Similarly, Apple didn't invent the smartphone, but through multiple innovations they took a solution that was previously very difficult to use and delivered a product that everyone would find easy to operate, from two-year-olds to ninety-two-year-olds.

Through this, Apple drove the mass adoption of the smartphone market and built one of the world's largest organisations in history.

Wage increases continued, and innovations in financial markets delivered a significant transformation to people's lives in the latter stages of this period.

As personal credit was made available to the masses in the form of loans and credit cards, financing and growth of investment wealth drove the expansion of multiple industries and, on the surface, played a role in levelling society and bridging the wealth divide as business sectors grew and individuals were able to start businesses and prosper.

Ind 3.0_The Digital Revolution 1970–2016

This is the revolution of our time. It delivered innovations in electronics and automation, bringing forth the birth of the computer age and globalisation as the world became a much smaller place.

Progress came thick and fast during this time and delivered a wide range of technical solutions, many of which we now take for granted in our everyday lives.

As more and more aspects of our lives and jobs become digitised, the Digital Revolution has lived up to its name and has formed the basis of our current modern society.

Key Innovations

- **1971:** Intel launch the first single-chip microprocessors that will go on to lead the personal computer revolutions.

- **1971**: IBM launch their 8" floppy disk and disk drive, bringing a universal data format and portability of data storage.

- **1972:** Sees the launch of the first video game console called Magnavox Odyssey.

- **1973:** The first fibre optic communication systems are developed by Optelecom. This goes on to launch the technology that serves our high-speed broadband today.

- **1973:** The first cell phone call is made in the UK.

- **1975:** Bill Gates and Paul Allen found Microsoft.

- **1975:** Steve Sasson of Kodak invent the first Digital Camera.

- **1975:** Introduction of the Video Cassette and war between VHS and Betamax.

the future of us

- **1976:** Steve Jobs and Steve Wozniak founded Apple.

- **1977:** Home computers enter the market, targeted as affordable and accessible devices to access the future of computing.

- **1977:** The Atari Video Computer Game system is launched. It becomes one of the most popular games machines of its era.

- **1984:** Introduction of Satellite TV opens access to a vast choice of home entertainment.

- **1989:** Tim Berners Lee invents the World Wide Web as part of a project to connect the computers of Scientists and universities across the world. This forms the basis of the Internet protocol we now use every day.

- **1995:** The DVD is invented and released the following year, transforming the way we consume media.

- **1997:** IBM's supercomputer Deep Blue beats world chess champion, Gary Kasparov.

- **1997:** First publicly available speech recognition software developed by Dragon systems.

- **1998:** Engineers from MIT and the University of California create the first Quantum Computer (2-bit) that can be loaded with data and output a solution. A key step in the future of computing.

- **1999:** The term 'Internet of Things is coined by Kevin Ashton in a bid to draw attention to the opportunity of RFID (Radio Frequency Identification) devices and their exciting opportunities. Future collusion with cellular technologies and future data networks take the term into the mainstream. I will explain IoT in more detail later in the book

our time in history

- **1999:** Napster brings music streaming to the masses, beginning the Streaming Revolution and transforming the music industry.

- **2000:** Friends Reunited is launched, bringing one of the first social interaction applications and, some would argue, the template for all social media applications that followed.

- **2000:** GPS (global position satellite) access was made available outside of the US military, transforming the future of SAT NAV and location services on our smartphones.

- **2003:** The Human Genome Project is completed, bringing incredible benefits in science and disease prevention and cures. It also raises potential discrimination issues around the wider uses of the data in areas such as health insurance.

- **2004:** Web 2.0 arrives as the second generation of the Internet, moving from static web pages to provide richer content, more end-user interaction, and gives birth to social media interaction applications.

- **2004:** Mark Zuckerberg launches Facebook, and love it or hate it, it provides a contact for social interaction that has never been seen before, transforming our relationships and the way we keep in touch forever.

- **2005:** 3D printing goes mainstream as affordable home printing unites come to market.

- **2006:** Sony launches its first E-Readers using electronic paper.

- **2007:** Fitbit launches, kick-starting a health revolution as people target themselves to hit the magical 10k steps per day.

- **2008:** Tesla releases their first electric car, the Roadster, with its supercar beating 0 to 60 acceleration.

- **2008:** Virgin Media provides the first fibre broadband to homes, revolutionising the home broadband market and powering the next stages of the Revolution.

- **2009:** The launch of the cryptocurrency Bitcoin, which goes on to become one of the largest cryptocurrencies using blockchain technology.

- **2009:** CRISPR, a genome editing tool, makes it easier than ever to edit DNA – it brings massive progress in science.

- **2011:** Siri voice activation and assistant arrives on the iPhone 4s.

- **2012:** Netflix launches in the UK, calling an end to the video shop and birth of the TV and Film streaming services.

- **2014:** Artificial Intelligence Computer known as Eugene Goostman almost passes the Turing test when it convinces one of a panel of three people that it is a real person.

- **2014:** Google launch their Glass solutions, bringing one of the first consumer AR solutions to market.

- **2014:** Amazon launch Alexa, the first home voice assistant.

- **2014:** Tesla launch Autopilot, the first commercially available rudimentary self-driving technology.

- **2015:** Apple launch its first Apple Watch, which receives mixed opinions on its launch but quickly progresses to become the best-selling watch brand in the world in under two years, beating the Swiss at their own game and reaching a hundred million users by the end of 2020.

→ Societal Impacts

A period of rapid technological advances and innovations, coupled with a transforming financial sector, provided a platform for development and growth that led to significant societal transformation.

Innovation, progress, prosperity, and opportunity drove growth across pretty much every industry for a number of generations – everyone from the army of labour provided by the vast number of Baby Boomers to the educated and ambitious children of Generation X, and the Tech-Savvy Millennials making the most of digital technologies in every aspect of their lives, benefited.

We have three generations in the workforce during this time, all with very different views and priorities but with a traditionalist majority clearly leading the direction and charge.

Government bodies and corporations encouraged growth, and finance and funding continued to become more widely available to both businesses and individuals.

Homeownership and personal credit became widely available, and standards of living greatly improved as a result.

While growth was evident across many industries and the standards of living greatly increased, more innovations, from home computing, home entertainment, satellite TV, a vast range of domestic appliances, foreign holidays, and designer clothing, took our focus.

Though, there was a simmering question on the back burner. Who would pay for all of this?

The buy-now-pay-later generations were born, with the marketing message that you really could 'have it all' driving significant growth in the finance industry. Just like Henry

the future of us

Ford's innovative wage increases drove markets in his time, available credit now had the same effect.

These same available credit systems would, however, also bring some challenging downsides for many.

In bids for growth, higher-risk finance was made available to those that wanted it. Without a full appreciation of the costs, debts would spiral to uncontrollable levels for many who struggled to pay back loans or credit cards, presenting a challenge to learn from today as the cost of our digital lives increases.

This pattern of increased high-risk borrowing didn't falter following the buy-it-now generations.

Instead, it extended into the previously safer mortgage markets and saw the subprime mortgage market collapse and the subsequent credit crisis of 2007/8. These acted as a second sobering reminder that we really can 'have it all' provided we also pay for it.

Advances and innovations in telecommunication and the introduction of the modern computer powered much of this new growth which, in turn, would itself go on to be one of the biggest industries ever.

In time, computing would start the biggest societal transformation seen yet.

As machines in the early Revolution automated manpower, computers in this Third Revolution automated mind power.

Computing solutions progressed to be present in almost every process, technology, and industry, completely transforming our roles and place in the workplace.

As factories evolved, automation reached its next stage with the introduction of Robotics.

Robots became able to take over human positions in production line processes where processes were repeatable and predictable. This moved us from the automation of labour to the automation of skill.

The combination of computing and Robotic automation led to incredible efficiency and, as expected, did displace many workers in many industries. But as with previous stages of the Revolution, these improvements went on to increase productivity and ultimately drove greater numbers of employment overall.

Workers up-skilled to build, programme, and maintain modern machines and Robots and, as a result, a more computer-literate generation emerged.

Organisations invested in up-skilling their workforces to operate and maintain these new machines, and computer studies and computer science classes were introduced to the education systems as governments recognised the growing importance of these skillsets.

The introduction of home computing and the birth of the Internet started a home computing revolution. With this, advances in mobile communication and computing led to the incredible smartphones and tablets we use every day.

These are now the remote controls to our lives, connecting us to everything and everyone.

The continuous drive for growth and profits did lead to some very bad habits, and there were some slips in working conditions.

A nonsense culture of 'greed is good' became the zeitgeist of the 80s and 90s after being popularised in movies. Similarly, whether or not they were aware of it, workers slipped into ideologies of 'first in the office, last to leave' and were blindsided back to pre-nine-to-five working hours.

This was later fuelled even further by technology; mobile devices allowed work to follow us home. Many sat with laptops perched on knees on sofas late into the evenings, and a culture of instant replies, regardless of the hour, became expected.

While we consider the early stages of the Industrial Revolution as incomparable to our lives of today, imagine flipping that around and showing those in the 1800s how automation ultimately progressed.

A lot has happened in the last 200 years.

→ **Learning & Observations**

The rapid growth of technology and the constant advent of new innovations resulted in the emergence of whole new industries that, in time, would quickly become some of the world's biggest brands. The same thing might happen again in future if we look at the growth in current new innovation sectors.

What does the future of the AI industry look like, for example?

It likely holds the same promise, if not more, than the early stages of computerisation. If capitalism dragged us back to old working habits, the driver for profit really has no brakes.

As we rebalance our lives on the back of Covid, how do we ensure we don't slip back again and ensure our work-life balance and well-being are our priority?

And further, what role will technology and innovation play in ensuring this?

Furthermore, as the cost of our modern digital lives grows, how can we learn from the previous credit crunch?

Sure, we have many things available to us, and we can 'have it all' – but that doesn't mean we should.

Furthermore, how do we keep this in balance as more things are digitised, and almost everything comes with a digital cost?

How we earn a living in the digital future is also likely to change, everything from industry progression to societal attitudes towards work. We are moving from 'buy now, pay later' toward a 'Life As A Service' generation. I will touch on this in more detail in a later chapter.

Ind 4.0_ Fourth Industrial Revolution 2016–Today

In 2016, Karl Schwab of the World Economic Forum heralded that we are now entering the Fourth Industrial Revolution. This is recognised and embraced across many industries, most commonly known as Industry 4.0 or the Disruption Revolution.

These titles recognise the rapid advancements in a number of key disruptive innovations, such as ubiquitous mobile super-computing, advanced Robotics, self-driving cars, neuro-technology, and genetic editing.

To this, I would also add these further innovations and developments in fields such as quantum computing, Augmented, Virtual, and Extended Reality, 5G connectivity and the growth of the Internet of Things, Smart Cities, and nanotechnologies.

Schwab is far from alone in his views and opinions; many are in total agreement. Many experts make these technologies and their societal impacts a key focus of their research as we all begin to explore the current Fourth Industrial Revolution.

The Fourth Industrial Revolution builds on the inventions and progress of the Third Industrial Revolution.

It is driven by a constant/progressive arrival of new innovations and a range of new and disruptive technologies and, when combined with existing technologies, results in the delivery of some truly incredible transformations and a promise of the ground-breaking possibilities ahead.

'Tomorrow holds promise beyond today.'

Key Innovations

- **2016:** Boston Dynamic reveal their canine-inspired Spot Robot.

- **2016:** TikTok launches with the platform suggesting our attention span will be between twenty-one and thirty-four seconds in the future. And while that might be the case, many now lose hours scrolling through these short video clips.

- **2016:** HTC launch their Vive VR Headset aimed at high-end PC users looking to explore the work of Virtual Reality and game in these new environments.

the future of us

- **2016:** Alpha Go AI Super-computer beats the world's best Go player.

- **2016:** Microsoft launch HoloLens, one of the first commercially available AR solutions aimed at commercial AR solutions.

- **2016:** Tesla announce Neuralink. Here, a high-bandwidth brain-machine interface connects humans and computers, holding the promise of delivering a medical wonder tool able to cure some cases of paralysis and solve a range of brain injuries and wider neurological conditions.

- **2017:** Microsoft Teams replaces the earlier Lync and Skype solutions following an internal company hackathon. This solution would go on to see daily use across every industry and provide the backbone of communications in the Future Of Work for many.

- **2017:** Narrowband IoT (Internet of Things) connectivity launches in the UK, allowing battery-powered 'things' to be connected to the Internet. Everything from sensors to parcels; pretty much everything can be connected and located.

- **2017:** Replika Ai launches, providing a text-based chatbot companion via users' smartphones. A very basic albeit very similar version of Scout but focused more on friendship than taking on our day jobs

- **2018:** Magic Leap launches their Business-focused AR headset, encouraging organisations to redefine how we access screens and visualise data.

- **2018:** Google Duplex Artificial Intelligence computer takes on the Turing test to successfully book a table in a restaurant and makes a hair styling appointment, fooling the person who answered the call that it was a real person.

our time in history

- **2018:** Synthesia Demo one of the first Deep Synthetic photorealistic Avatars using ComputerVision AI and Script engines to recreate a highly realistic avatar of us in digital form. I will expand on Avatars later in the book.

- **2019:** 5G launches in the UK, bringing sight of the possible future of high-speed connectivity without wires as excited consumers enjoy the increased speeds but with its real opportunities lying in industrial machines, automation, and drones.

- **2019:** Tesla announce the Tesla bot. Is this the body of Scout? Artificial Intelligence to not only organise our lives but to tidy up after us as well? I'm in!!

- **2020:** Facebook/Oculus launch their Quest 2 VR headset aimed at the consumer market, untethering consumer VR from high-spec PCs and becoming affordable to the masses.

- **2020:** Deep-Fake AI is capable of cloning human voice, presenting a world of opportunity and concern in equal measure.

- **2020:** Open AI launches GPT3. It is one of the largest and most powerful language processing models ever created. It has 175 billion parameters and the ability to generate human-like text and perform a wide range of language-based tasks, such as translation, summarisation, and answering questions. Give it a try at **chat.openai.com** Could this be the power behind my fictional companion Scout…? And how long now before she's given her voice? If of interest give the 2013 Film 'Her' a try to see the art of the possible for a future version of Scout.

- **2022:** Facebook change their name to Meta, clearly calling the company's future focus and a direction to invest in the Metaverse.

- **2022:** IBM unveil their Osprey Quantum Computer, with their fastest Quantum processor to date packing 433 qubits. Able to solve complex computations over a hundred million times faster that even the most advanced super computers of today.

- **2022:** DALLE 2 Text-to-Image AI launches to the public, allowing public access for people to generate and create images and artwork from a description using natural language. Give it a try at **www.openai.com/dall-e-2/**

→ **Societal Impacts**

As we come to the end of the current pandemic, it's clear to see we are currently living through a fairly significant period of change.

In the same way we listened to people working twelve-hour days six days a week in history lessons, so too will our time also make the subject of future history lessons.

Children will be told stories of how we used to wake early, cram ourselves onto trains and motorways, sit behind desks in an office for eight-plus hours, often to email someone sitting next to us, and repeat this pattern five days a week.

The children of tomorrow will simply ask, "*Why*?"

The onset of the global pandemic and subsequent lockdowns forced us to work and communicate in new ways.

With it came the realisation that we can work differently.

We began to question our old 'traditional' working practices and challenged our old work-life balance as we adjusted to our new ways of working. We realised there was another way, and people embraced the long-overdue opportunity for change.

This time, the change is mainly driven by people.

Zoom, FaceTime, and Teams are not new technologies. They've been around for many years. We didn't desert the office upon their invention – it took the pandemic to pause our plans and to show us the capability and opportunity these technologies could bring to drive real, long-term change.

The pandemic gave us more time, and we used this to get fit.

We bought home workout equipment and hit the street with our smart watches tracking our progress and health. We joined digital communities in a bid to gain social interaction, and we tried new technologies, such as Virtual Reality, to digitally transport ourselves to new locations as the Government locked us down.

With progressions in technology, competitive markets, and regulation, we live and work in pretty decent conditions compared to our ancestors. Yet we are far from perfect, and many would agree we still have a way to go – particularly in terms of work-life balance and wider Digital Inclusion.

I lead several teams of experts who possess skills they could not learn in the education system, mainly because the roles they do didn't exist when they were in school.

Furthermore, these technologies are so new we are still learning many of them ourselves. As technology quickly advances, many industries are impacted by the need for self-development and up-skilling and place this high on their agendas. Those with these skills are in high demand in the jobs market today.

Employment is at an all-time high, and the question of whether work is a choice rather than a necessity for many is now rife as organisation struggle to find people to fill their vacancies.

In some cases, they are even struggling to maintain services and operations due to staff shortages.

Also has our welfare system lost or changed its purpose?

Is it now providing a way of life as an alternative to work for many?

While the rise of Digital Technologies aids and improves the lives of many, it also drives a significant level of divide across society in the form of Digital Inclusion. The cost of digital devices, connectivity, and applications prevents many people and children from gaining access to technology.

In turn, this restricts education and the social interaction needed to be present and included in our modern world. We see many private organisations taking very positive steps to address the Digital Divide, but for me, personally, this needs further and significant government intervention to address and close.

Disruptive headlines bring news of robots taking over our jobs or even the world.

Robots and artificial intelligence solutions are used everywhere, from call centres to retail applications. As organisations begin to look at how tasks can be automated through AI to improve customer services and reduce costs, workers are beginning to be displaced.

We also lost our children to technology.

Sounds dramatic but playing outside with jumpers for goalposts and biking through the streets is a thing of the past. Now our children enter their immersive world of social gaming, donning their headsets and interacting digitally for many hours at a time.

We have moved from negotiating home time to negotiating screen time, from standing at the front door calling our children inside to standing at their bedroom door calling them to go outside.

We talk less, and we chat more. As we understand the power of technology, we expect far more from the services we interact and engage with – from public services to how we pay bills.

We don't want to sit in call queues; we want to self-serve or use a chat box to quickly answer queries or issues. We don't want to wait for anything! As we grow into the instant generation, next-day delivery becomes today.

We want to be predicted, and we are prepared to trade more information in return for better services.

And as energy prices rise and we consider the growing number of digital direct debits leaving our accounts, we raise an eyebrow of concern at how the cost of our digital lives may unfold.

Rising inflation and the increased cost of living is a simmering concern and is likely to bring further rebalance to people's lives. Can we have it all? Or will we have to cut our cloth and find out what is truly needed and important in the future?

As this stage brings us to our present day, it's difficult to understand what stage of the journey we find ourselves in; we have no end date as of yet.

Technology has certainly paved the way for potential change, but I'd say that while progress to date has been considerable and, in some cases, incredible, it has yet to reach its full power in transforming our lives.

I describe our current stage as a phase of trial and 'proof of concept'. A period of testing, trialling, and developing. Some things will fail, some things will fly, and the likely decider of the outcomes will be us.

In the early stages of the Industrial Revolution, innovation and capitalism drove change, but the biggest catalyst for our generation's transformation will be us. How we respond (to embrace technology or make changes to how we use it morally and ethically) and the stance we take on certain aspects will be crucial to the outcome.

I still stand by the principle that resistance is futile.

If technology has a benefit, it will naturally surface despite our views or opinions. However, different from our ancestors, today, our collective voices are far stronger, and the decisions we make as a society will therefore play a significant role in our technological development rather than having no choice but to constantly adapt as with previous generations.

This, for me, is as much a People Revolution as it is a Technology Revolution.

→ **Learning & Observations**

Regardless of your age, we are all currently living through a period of truly unprecedented transformation. The pandemic forced an instant and complete evolution of how and where we work. We've quickly adapted to use new technologies to transform our working practices, and for many, it brought into question their current work-life balance and the overall purpose of what they do for a living and who they do it for, as the Great Resignation continues across every industry.

While this period to date will be marked down in history as we move from patterns of work that have remained unchanged for almost a hundred years, we've quickly and quietly adapted to the changes. Thankfully, the range of technologies needed to work, communicate, and shop remotely was already available, so every generation was able to embrace them. Overall, we became pretty efficient in the process.

So, as we pause for breath, we look to headlines of the Great Resignation, the Future Of Work, and the Rise of Machines as they take over our jobs.

This chapter, coupled with our own recent experiences, reminds us to expect the unexpected as history documents that no one is immune to change as we consider the questions of what and where next.

The rapidly growing, and continuous introduction, of new disruptive technologies holds the promise of considerable future transformation. Many of us are at a crossroads in looking forward to these transformations but are also still attempting to understand and manage the technologies of today; things have become a little confusing and overwhelming.

As we are still in the infancy of this stage of the Revolution, we are still learning our lessons. I feel there are several points we should consider as we navigate our own stage in the journey.

As we've explained, Robots taking our jobs is nothing new, but advances in innovations such as Artificial

Intelligence and Machine Learning are likely to bring a new aspect of transformation during our time.

Robots have previously automated physical processes; these new technologies will automate the power of the mind, moving the focus from manual to mental agility as Robots take over more administrative duties and professions.

Much of what we learn in school today will be done by a machine in the future.

These initially mind-blowing technologies, like Chat GPT3, hold promises of not only considerable capabilities but are also highly likely to completely transform life as we know it. Without a doubt, they will certainly impact how we live and work over the remainder of our careers and lifetimes ahead.

So, how to evolve to learn new skills or gain a better understanding of these technologies to work with Robots?

The rise of these technologies will transform industries, and, as we've seen, organisations don't always fully appreciate the power of disruption.

We've also learnt here that many of these initially incredible innovations are not all one-way juggernauts of growth. Their initial innovations need to be backed by great business leadership to ride the waves of future change.

As Facebook and Uber remind us, it's not always plain sailing.

Finally, we must ask: 'What is the current and future cost of our digital lives?'

As we considered in the last section, we are moving from a 'buy now, pay later' to a 'Things/Life As A Service' model. But this is now coupled, in the Fourth Revolution, with disruptions of working practices and industries and a rapidly rising cost of living combined with growing inflation, energy prices, and interest rates.

History reminds us that these patterns are often not short-lived. The question to consider is who will pay for our increasingly digital lives if we can't?

We have a lot to consider and what is becoming abundantly clear is that things are speeding up, and it's all becoming a little confusing.

Summary & Where Next?

As we stand back to look over the last 250 years, the Industrial, Technical, and Digital Revolutions hold consistent and constant themes of change.
The continuous advent of new technology has completely transformed how people live and work forever.
But technological inventions, while significant, have only been driven to mass adoption or delivered real change through the further innovation of others.
We've moved from farmers to influencers, from distant to connected, from physical to remote, as innovation has touched and transformed every industry.
It has even created new industries and services that we now can't imagine our lives without.
While it's almost impossible to compare our lives today with those of our ancestors – and it's easy to raise an eyebrow at the reality of some of the possible mind-boggling future technologies – our one constant is change.
As history has a habit of repeating itself, we can learn much from the past as we plan and navigate our futures.

Take Aways & Points to Consider

- We are not the first generations to live through change.

- As history has a habit of repeating itself, what can we learn from these previous transformations and disruptions?

- Change and disruption will not announce itself and it may not have your best interests at heart. It will disrupt the lives of the unprepared.

- Start to consider how technology and innovations are already transforming your industry, job role, hobbies and interests and life in general. How could you learn more about the basics of these? We'll explore these closer in Chapter 8

*'If Technology is the vehicle for change,
and Innovation is the fuel
Society is now the driver.'*

3
why our time will be different

'The future is faster than you think.'
Peter Diamandis

So, history tells us change is nothing new, and it's inevitable that future transformation is ahead; it's simply our time to face it. However, this then leaves us to ask what the future has in store for us, and how our time might be different.

While there's no crystal ball to know for sure, we can look to the possibilities and potential of the new innovative and disruptive technologies that gave the Fourth Industrial Revolution its name.

This, combined with evidence of the significant transformations of the last ten or fifteen years, the recurring patterns and trends of progress and transformation of the last 250 years, and our changing societal attitudes, asks us to consider what we do and who we work with and for as we look to technology to better support our digital lives.

As businesses, we make decisions on the future based on trends, experiences, and data – and this is the insight that provides us with a good starting point as individuals to now pause, and consider our own 'where next?'

So now, let's look at some of the driving factors of change in more detail. We will look at those most likely to accelerate our journeys into the future and, crucially, why.

Pace of Change

'Progress so far will look like a dress rehearsal compared to the progress ahead.'

If we look back again at the collective timeline of technological innovation in the **Technology Growth Acceleration** graph, it's clear to see that things are speeding up.

In the early stages of the Revolution, it was driven by a limited number of key technologies that, while significant in their impact and transformation, took time to progress and adapt.

Gradually, they transformed industries and, in turn, lives.

the future of us

Technology Growth Acceleration

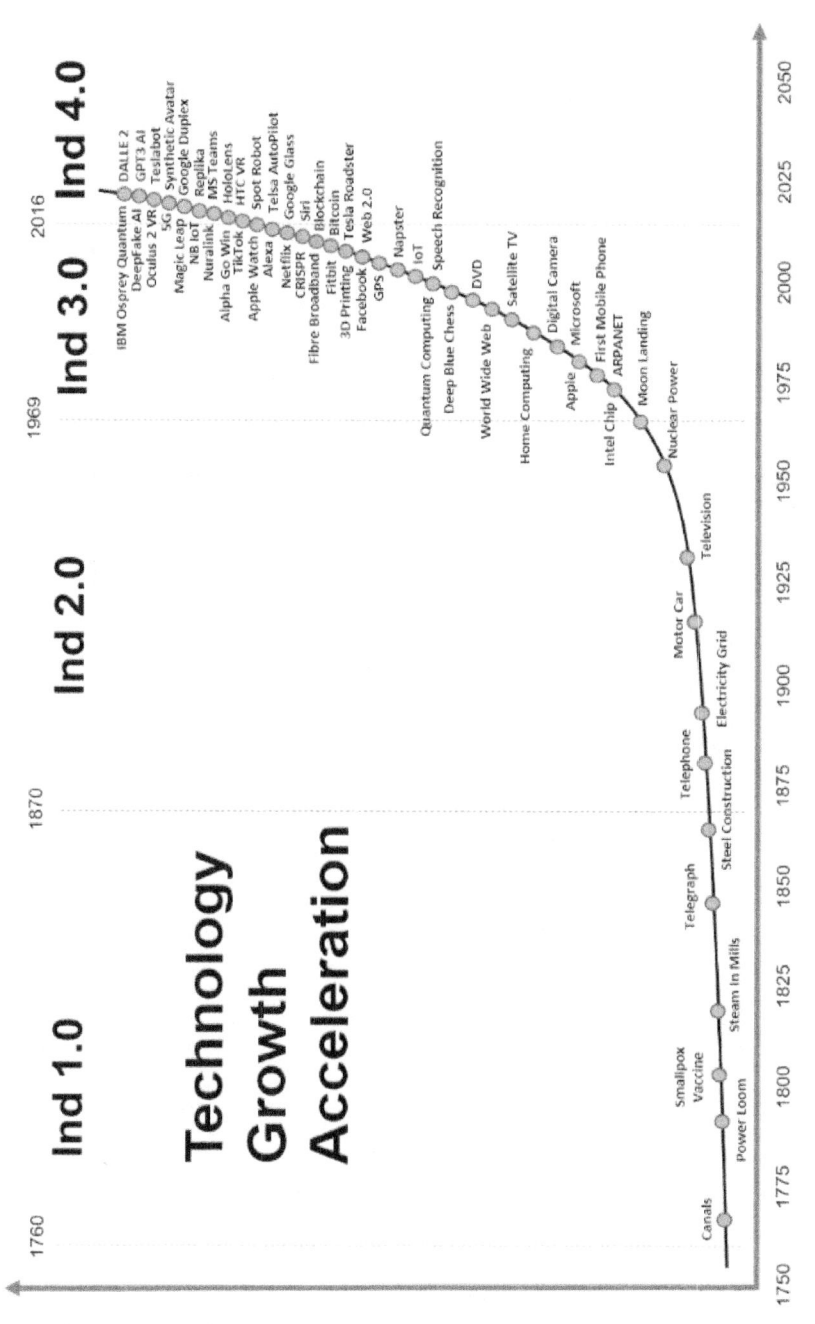

Ind 1.0 — 1760 / 1870
Ind 2.0
Ind 3.0 — 1969
Ind 4.0 — 2016

Timeline events:
- Canals
- Power Loom
- Smallpox Vaccine
- Steam In Mills
- Telegraph
- Steel Construction
- Telephone
- Electricity Grid
- Motor Car
- Television
- Nuclear Power
- Moon Landing
- ARPANET
- Intel Chip
- First Mobile Phone
- Apple
- Microsoft
- Digital Camera
- Home Computing
- Satellite TV
- World Wide Web
- DVD
- Deep Blue Chess
- Speech Recognition
- Quantum Computing
- IoT
- Napster
- GPS
- Facebook
- Web 2.0
- 3D Printing
- Bitcoin
- Fibre Broadband
- Blockchain
- CRISPR
- Siri
- Netflix
- Google Glass
- Apple Watch
- Telsa AutoPilot
- Alexa
- Spot Robot
- TikTok
- HoloLens
- Alpha Go Win
- HTC VR
- Nuralink
- MS Teams
- NB IoT
- Replika
- Magic Leap
- Google Duplex
- 5G
- Synthetic Avatar
- Oculus 2 VR
- Teslabot
- DeepFake AI
- GPT3 AI
- IBM Osprey Quantum
- DALLE 2

Timeline: 1750, 1775, 1800, 1825, 1850, 1875, 1900, 1925, 1950, 1975, 2000, 2025, 2050

All images are also available to view and download at **www.futureofus.co.uk**

Around the 1970s, this pattern sharply increased as the progression of technology in the Third Industrial Revolution brought with it the birth of computing and a pattern of growth known as Moore's Law.

Gordon Moore was an engineer and executive working at Intel in the 1970s when he noticed a pattern and predicted that computer processing chips would double in power, shrink in size, and reduce in price every couple of years.

He was right.

This pattern has pretty much run throughout the evolution of microchips to date, which has powered a mass of other solutions and appliances and has experienced a period of exponential growth in which they doubled in performance.

Many are now quoting that Moore's law has run its course as the size of microchips is reaching its physical limits. And while that may be factually correct, this pattern of progress still continues.

Now, however, it is now driven by a wider combination of progressions in technology innovations and, further, our changing attitudes around how we use Digital Solutions to both work smarter and live better.

While we've seen many new technologies drive some incredible transformation, it's been alongside the luxury of time. We could either embrace them as early adopters, or sit back, observe, and learn more as we subtly adapted to allow these new technologies to become just another part of our daily lives.

We are not the first generations to notice these patterns and trends of acceleration, nor the first to use the past to prepare for the future.

Way before Moore, in 1942, Austrian economist Joseph Schumpeter coined the term 'creative destruction' to describe the effects of innovation disruption and opportunity in industry.

He described this as a cycle of waves, with each wave building in momentum, delivering more change over a shorter period of time. This pattern continues way beyond his time right up to our present day, therefore proving his theory as the pattern grows and builds in momentum.

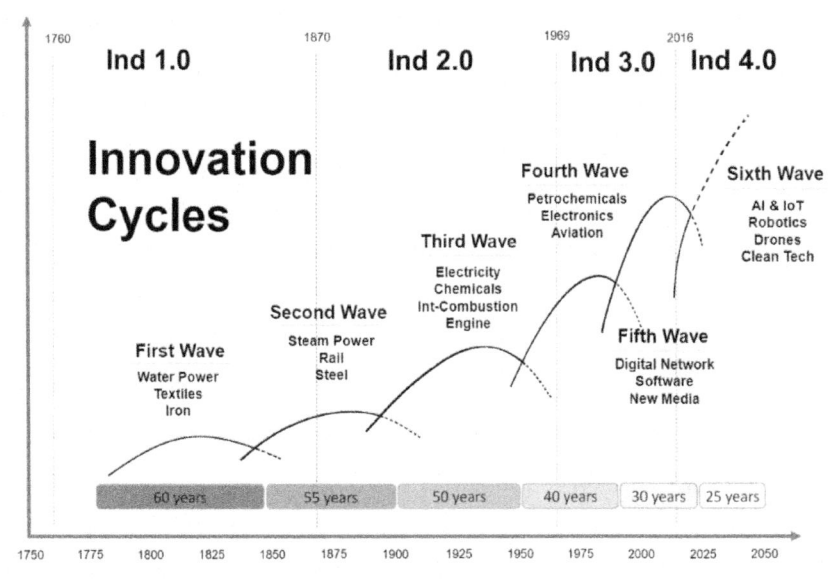

Innovation Cycles

Ind 1.0 (1760)	Ind 2.0 (1870)	Ind 3.0 (1969)	Ind 4.0 (2016)
First Wave – Water Power, Textiles, Iron	Second Wave – Steam Power, Rail, Steel	Third Wave – Electricity, Chemicals, Int-Combustion Engine	Fourth Wave – Petrochemicals, Electronics, Aviation / Fifth Wave – Digital Network, Software, New Media / Sixth Wave – AI & IoT, Robotics, Drones, Clean Tech

60 years | 55 years | 50 years | 40 years | 30 years | 25 years

1750 1775 1800 1825 1850 1875 1900 1925 1950 1975 2000 2025 2050

All images are also available to view and download at www.futureofus.co.uk

And again, as businesses, we plan and build based on market trends, facts, and, wherever possible, hard data. This, for me, summarises and validates our direction of travel as individuals as we all now enter the Sixth Wave of the Innovation Cycle.

This pattern of growth and change is widely recognised and acknowledged by industry analysts, experts, and Futurists alike, with many relaying that the wave is actually building far faster and steeper than many are fully prepared for.

> 'We are likely to see more transformation
> over the next 20 years
> than we have in the last 300 years.'
> **Gerd Leonhard – Futurist**

My awareness of this trend (coupled with my daily experiences of working and researching new technologies and noticing some other accelerating factors that I will cover here) is one of the reasons I wrote this book.

As the pattern grows day by day and we consider that we are not all experts in technology, there's a growing sense that things are starting to feel a little uncomfortable.

This occurs as the constant advent of seemingly endless new innovations land in our lives or appear on the horizon, leaving many either nervously ignoring them or simply hoping we might avoid too much disruption in our careers and lifetimes.

Or, as up until now, we just sort of hope we will adapt and get used to them.

Well, hope and luck aren't the best business strategies, and nor will they be for our own futures. Instead, we need to acknowledge that we're now on the wave, and it's a steep one – we need to learn to surf. And fast!

Technology Advances

As we look at some of the incredible technology already supporting our lives today, from our mobile remote controls to the supercomputers beating chess champions or that are ready to drive our car, it's sometimes difficult to consider how we could possibly deliver more from technology.

Surely, we've hit a peak?

In 1899, the Commissioner of the US Patent Office, Charlie H Duell, stated that 'everything that can be invented has been invented' which was clearly apocryphal but was perhaps stated as more of a reflection of the sentiment at the time – considering the incredible progress made to that point.

Now, quietly in the background, the Innovators, Developers, Scientists, Creatives, and Entrepreneurs continue their work to bring us the next Mega Trends of progress and wonder. They are busy designing and developing a whole range of progressive solutions that will likely appear in our lifetimes and bring significant transformation.

• • •

Mega Trends of Our Time

I referenced a few of these innovations in the Story of Scout, and here I want to touch quickly on a few of the key technologies that are likely to impact our lives.

Also, I want to stress that we don't need to be experts in all these fields; we just need to demystify the terminology and understand the basics of what they do and how they will/might impact our lives. I will cover more on how we do this in Chapter 8.

VR *(Virtual Reality)*

As explained in the Story of Scout, VR is a full immersive solution where we place a headset on and leave the physical world in full and totally immerse ourselves in a Virtual Reality.

VR has been desperately trying to find a use case for mass adoption since its creation in the 70s.

Currently used in niche fields such as training courses, therapy, virtual meetings, and gaming, the overall uptake is still very low due to the costs and limited range of available solutions. However, this will likely change as we see considerable investments in the development of VR hardware and software by both the main tech companies and start-ups.

Progress will likely cross over into wider applications such as virtual workplace meetings, TV and media, and gaming. Despite questions over its realities, as the cost of equipment decreases or VR experiences improve, I do feel it's likely to play an increasingly important role in the Future Of Work.

→ **Impact on our lives**

VR is one to watch as it continues to look for niche solutions for both entertainment and work. It will be limited by the reality of wearing a headset for long periods of time, but it will be great for short, interactive, and more immersive activities.

VR's focus on entertainment and gaming is likely to make it more mainstream.

While we might not spend whole days in VR, I do feel organisations will likely use VR as a bridging technology in a more remote and hybrid world. But a great device at a low price point will be required to really allow us to make the most of the VR possibilities and to allow us to really travel without moving.

Metaverse

The digital virtual locations we enter in VR are often collectively referred to as the Metaverse. This is a term penned in a 90's Sci-Fi novel called *Snow Crash* by Neal Stephenson. The term stuck and Facebook changing their name to Meta suggest the focus of their intentions for the future.

We can pretty much build any environment in the Metaverse, either replicating a physical location, such as a museum, city, office, or school or creating a virtual world from our own imaginations that we can visit and explore simply by placing our VR headsets on.

From the comfort of our sofas, we will see everything digitised and mirrored in a virtual environment.

In theory, there will be a digital twin of every service or location. Due to the immersive and engaging nature of VR, you, in theory, surrender your attention from the outside world and focus purely on what is directly in front and around you.

In VR, there is no distraction from your phone, emails, or a message. Therefore, Metaverse environments will likely be used to fully engage people in education, more advanced training requirements or important business projects.

We will also see a dedicated focus on other niche services, from gaming and media to adult entertainment.

→ **Impact on our lives**

We will likely see a digital twin of every possible location, from businesses replicating their entire organisations and using Metaverse platforms to allow a more immersive digital experience for virtual visits or meetings.

Through to allowing us to explore an entire city remotely before you visit to plan your trip or simply to visit a new environment such as an office, school, or health centre remotely to familiarise ourselves with a layout in advance of a visit.

We will also see digital twins for a wide range of other locations, such as concert venues and sports stadiums.

But demand will be dictated by the progress and adoption of VR.

AR (Augmented Reality)

As described in the Story of Scout, AR Glass technology sits somewhere between the Metaverse and the real world. Using Glass, you will stay in the physical world; however, a range of AR Glass solutions will provide a digital overlay of information in a kind of 3D experience.

Due to both the use case and the monetisation opportunity, this technology is likely to be a game changer and very big news in the Future Of Us for three key reasons.

Firstly, it's likely to become our First Field of View, providing us with the alternative options of glancing at our watch or phone screen to seeing notifications appear in our peripheral vision.

Secondly, beyond simply sending you notifications, these solutions will interact with a whole host of other solutions and services in the IoT space as more and more things become connected.

As an example, holding your gaze on an item in a store or tapping the arm of your glasses could instantly provide you with information or make you aware of an offer to entice you to buy it. Also, if you were visiting a new city, you could use Glass technology to provide you with precise directions and a range of options along the route, such as the nearest coffee shop or toilets.

These possibilities – coupled with changing attitudes towards data sharing – will transform the world of marketing completely. We will control the level of information we see, and these tiny screens will become the hottest marketing space available.

Finally, AR will also improve and interact with a range of existing solutions in our homes, such as making 3D TV a reality and improving 3D interactivity in video calls.

Just imagine your colleague popping out of your next video call in a 3D head and shoulders view!

Some are suggesting that Glass may eventually replace our mobile phones. As explained in the Story of Scout, while I don't rule it out completely, I think phones will continue to provide the power behind Glass solutions to keep the size down and also as means of manual input for some time to come.

We will likely see a few big-bang launches over the years ahead by the main technology companies as they compete for this Third, but soon to be First, Field of View.

→ Impact on our lives

Put simply; it's going to be MASSIVE! All the levers, drivers, and collisions of technology are falling into place to make this a reality and a significant solution in so many aspects of our lives.

There are big prizes associated with the monetisation of AR, and we will see considerable investment to help make this a reality.

Due to the improvements it will bring to our lives, I predict that while it might have a slow initial build and lots of regulation pushback around privacy, overall, this will likely have significant societal appeal and be one of the most transformative technologies of all time as Sci-Fi meets reality, and the digital and physical worlds collide.

XR (Mixed or Extended Reality)

There are several descriptions for what XR is but put simply: it's where AR and VR meet.

Imagine you are totally immersed in VR and blocked out from the real world but have the option to clearly see your physical environment at the flick of a switch. This option to dual task will likely see high-end niche tech solutions aimed at industries such as construction, design, and manufacturing.

While many suggest AR will replace XR over time, I think AR will be about lightweight and non-intrusive devices, while VR and XR will require a bit more grunt and bigger, more powerful devices for some time to come.

→ Impact on our lives

XR is a natural progression of both AR and VR, really, and could have some interesting use cases in education, gaming, and business training. XR will also likely play a role in how we work with Robots in the future.

The big tech giants will race to capture both our Third Field of Notification and what will likely become the 'Window To Work' for the large majority of us. Expect to see new VR, AR and XR headsets and glasses arriving very soon.

Avatars

As our worlds become more virtual, so too must we.

With VR, we enter virtual worlds using headsets but can't also send a video image of ourselves. Instead, we send a digitally recreated version called an avatar.

We have two options. We can build a lifelike representation of ourselves using photos or video images to recreate a virtual version of us, or we can build a completely new version of ourselves that allows us to either enhance our image or create something totally whacky – anything from an animal to a superhero version of ourselves.

We can be anything we want to be in a virtual world, and the anonymity of an alternative avatar will appeal to many. Advanced AI technologies, such as Deep Synthetics, will also allow us to pre-film HD replicas of ourselves from which AI can recreate avatars of us so realistic many will be hard-pressed to know it's not actually us.

Think of the celebrity Deep Fakes. It's the same thing, but hopefully with your clothes on. These will also likely be used in video communications in cases where we can't send our real image, such as while we're travelling.

→ **Impact on our lives**

We will gradually compile a library of avatars that we'll use to join a number of different VR solutions, tweaking and enhancing this over time.

We will go on to build very realistic replicas of ourselves and customise everything from the way we look to the clothes we wear and the items our avatars own via NFTs (see next section). Initially, these may feel a little gimmicky, but they will improve through the addition of lip-syncing and gesture replication and we'll gradually grow more comfortable with them.

Why bother getting dressed for a video call when we can send a virtual version of ourselves instead?

NFTs (Non-Fungible Tokens)

Basically, these are digital items or assets in a virtual world. They might be items our avatars wear, such as a watch or branded clothing, or they may be a piece of artwork, a car, a piece of land in a virtual platform or world, or even another avatar.

Whatever it is, it will either be unique in its existence or limited to a set number of versions. We will own the digital rights to these items, but as we can't physically touch them, we will own them through a digital ledger called a Blockchain (next section) to prove ownership and authenticity.

Applications will allow us to see and manage our digital items and enable us to sell or trade them.

→ Impacts on our lives

These are already very big businesses as people rush to purchase clothing brands for their avatars in virtual environments or to own digital artworks. Values soared to some incredible prices and then fell sharply as people reassessed whether this was hype or reality.

I predict the majority of us will customise items in our virtual environments with a degree of novelty while watching the reality of the value of digital items and their trading environments over time.

Blockchain

Blockchain is a system and method of recording information in a way that makes it very difficult, if not impossible, to hack or beat.

It uses a network of computers to act as a digital ledger of transactions and authentication. If you were to buy something right now, your bank card would directly check with your bank that you have the funds. Then, the bank will instantly decline or approve via a clearing system.

This is a single transaction that someone could hack and pretend they are you. In a Blockchain, however, it could hold that same information across ten different computers and instantly check if this information is correct.

The neat part is that if someone tried to hack this and pretend they were you, they would have to hack all ten computers at exactly the same time and know the agreed keys for each, making this almost impossible to hack or beat.

Behind the scenes, the information it shares in this disturbed ledger would be encrypted, so we wouldn't see each other's information. Instead, our computers would act as a step or process in the wider validation, constantly updating each other to maintain the chain.

→ **Impact on our lives**

The use cases form a long list, and the technology is already working in a number of solutions in our lives and will bring some significant impacts; however, the reality is that we probably won't even notice it.

Blockchain will simply increase the security of our applications, our personal data, and the data people hold on us and allow us to make transactions in new and far safer ways.

This will massively reduce, if not totally eradicate several frauds.

IoT (Internet of Things)

This term refers to anything that is connected in order to provide information. The world is connected by millions of things, from a vending machine telling the supplier it's running low on a specific product to your smart meter telling your energy provider exactly how much power you've consumed.

This is far from new technology; billions of things — from our cars to our phones — are all connected and interacted with across the world.

Until recently, devices could only be connected if they had a power supply, which greatly limited what we could communicate with. However, technologies have evolved to allow us to connect very small and moving assets via small batteries.

Imagine being able to track your children's gym bag or an item you ordered online from the second it's dispatched to delivery. Or to look at an item on the shelf in a store and then see more information on your AR glasses' lenses as the two services interoperate.

A richer example of IoT in practice is city centre car parking. Here, sensors are placed in the parking space, and you can then book empty spaces using your phone, use your sat nav to find it, and then pay for the time you were parked there instantly.

→ Impact on our lives

IoT will play an increasingly important role in the future as more things become interconnected to improve the services and information they generate.

IoT is already very mature, but the collision of technologies in AR and data sharing is endless; the monetisation of these interactions will see constant and significant improvements.

The commercial growth of this market is huge, and IoT will enable a far broader range of solutions and applications, making this a big focus for many Innovators and tech giants. Apple's Air Tags are a great consumer use case already available.

If something can be connected in the future, it probably will be.

•••

Artificial Intelligence (AI)

AI is the development of computer systems to be able to perform tasks that would normally require human intelligence.

In theory, AI mimics human cognitive skills, such as decision-making, speech recognition, language translation, and image description. Its main functions are learning and problem-solving, either learning from its own mistakes or sorting through vast data files to solve problems far better and quicker than the human mind ever could.

Where previously machines replaced physical manpower, AI will now replace intelligent mind power

AI is tipped to bring the biggest transformation in the Future Of Us as it will provide the power behind many of the solutions we've covered in this chapter.

It's likely to bring a transformation to the Future Of Work beyond anything we can imagine today, with some experts calling out that AI will displace millions of jobs leading to an employment and skill crisis.

Others suggest it may grow to such a point that it actually creates more jobs than it replaces, this will be heavily dependent on people's ability to retrain and learn the new skills required to work with and service the AI industry.

the future of us

AI is a complex field made up of a range of different computing machines broken down into three key areas (Narrow, General, and Super Intelligence) and four subcategories (Reactive, Limited Memory, Theory of Mind, and Self-Aware).

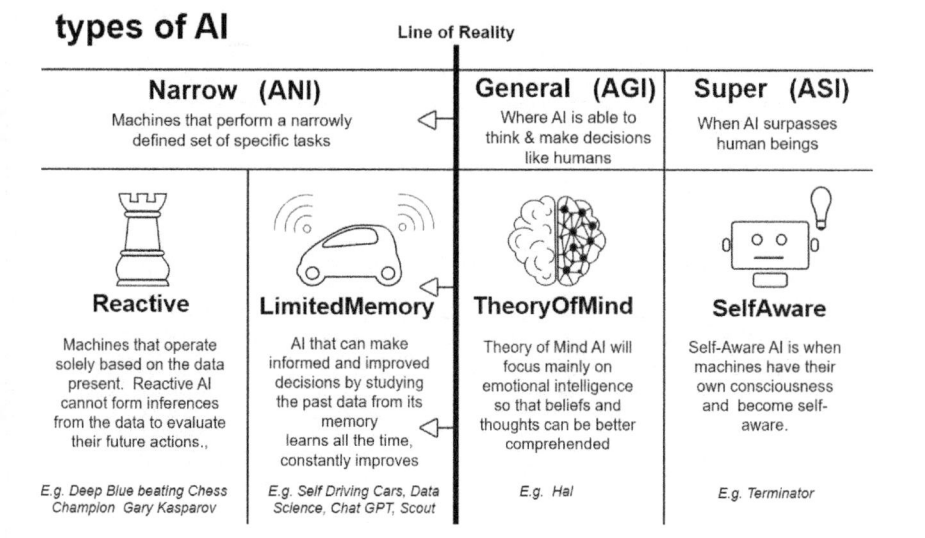

types of AI

Line of Reality

Narrow (ANI)	General (AGI)	Super (ASI)
Machines that perform a narrowly defined set of specific tasks	Where AI is able to think & make decisions like humans	When AI surpasses human beings

Reactive	LimitedMemory	TheoryOfMind	SelfAware
Machines that operate solely based on the data present. Reactive AI cannot form inferences from the data to evaluate their future actions.,	AI that can make informed and improved decisions by studying the past data from its memory learns all the time, constantly improves	Theory of Mind AI will focus mainly on emotional intelligence so that beliefs and thoughts can be better comprehended	Self-Aware AI is when machines have their own consciousness and become self-aware.
E.g. Deep Blue beating Chess Champion Gary Kasparov	E.g. Self Driving Cars, Data Science, Chat GPT, Scout	E.g. Hal	E.g. Terminator

All images are also available to view and download at www.futureofus.co.uk

Narrow Intelligence – Machine Learning

This is where we programme machines to carry out single or multiple but limited tasks. Already a mature and very progressive industry, Narrow AI has two subcategories – Reactive and Limited Memory.

1) Reactive AI

Machines perform a single task for a specific outcome, such as a computer beating a chess champion.

It's programmed to play chess millions of times very quickly and learns every possible move combination, and is then able to predict every possible outcome, meaning it's unbeatable by a human as the AI's memory and the speed it can recall and then play moves is far greater than that of a human.

Or in services like Netflix's recommendation engine, another example where it remembers your previous titles watched and searched and then looks up similar users' data to see who else watched it and what they went on to watch and enjoy afterwards.

It then makes similar recommendations to you and improves itself if the recommendation was successful or not (knowing if you actually watched it all or switched off early into watching).

Reactive AI cannot form inferences from the data to evaluate their future actions. It's programmed and operated solely to do exactly what we ask it to do, with the data we present it, with no or limited variation.

2) Limited Memory

The next progression, where AI trains itself using collated and live data to make decisions on the best outcomes.

It's programmed to learn and constantly improve itself over time, similar to how our minds work. This is where the learning part of Machine Learning comes in.

Such as a self-driving car that constantly reads its environment and then makes decisions based on the data and a range of possible outcomes. As it encounters an obstacle, it makes an instant decision based on whether it is best to swerve left or right to avoid it based on the data available at that precise moment and the success or failure of previous similar interventions.

Or in a call centre software system where the model trains itself to collate all the previous customer queries, asks, and all the possible outcomes and then suggests an answer to our queries, checking after every step to see if it got it right or not, and adjusting to improve as required.

And in AI solutions such as Chat GPT application are generative AI tools which allow users to enter questions and receive incredibly detailed and also humanlike text replies or content.

These types of AI are incorporated into a growing range of solutions that we use every day. And, while it's classed as 'narrow' because it's usually designed to perform limited tasks, it's considered intelligent to a degree because it learns from mistakes and successes, becoming more intelligent over time.

While they may focus on a single or limited task in many cases, completing multiple AI tasks and decisions, as with the Story of Scout, is where it will give the impression it is more intelligent than it currently is.

→ **Impact on our lives**

These two types of AI are in mass commercial development and probably already impacting your industry or role. As the race to sell AI As A Service takes off, you can bet someone somewhere is currently weighing up what you do and looking to see if they could train AI to do it faster and cheaper.

If a process is predictable and repeatable, then Reactive AI will likely be able to do it better, faster, cheaper, and safer than a human. If a role involves sorting vast amounts of data, spotting patterns, predicting outcomes, and then proactively solving problems, our human minds will be no match for limited AI.

Combined, their possibilities reach far and wide from Narrow AI suggesting replies to our emails, creating a mass of content in marketing or research projects and driving our cars, which, as the technologies progress and regulations evolve, hold the risk of displacing millions of workers in administrative, research, marketing and professional driving roles, from taxi drivers as explored in Scout to the millions of couriers and HGV drivers across the globe.

All of which will require no sleep, no lunch break, or a pension plan, as the question of *what if* moves to *what next*, as the risk of disruption now becomes very real and far closer.

In reality, these are the AI technologies that **will** replace many jobs over the years ahead. History reminds us that this is nothing new. And just as machines took jobs in the past, they will do the same during our time.

> **NOTE:** Before we continue, I want to draw your attention to the 'Line of Reality' in the diagram on page 95, clearly dividing these four areas.

To the right of this line is where it starts to get a bit scary and Sci-Fi.

To stress, Reactive and Limited Memory are here now and very real, whereas General and Super AI are still the focus of Developers and Scientists as they work on AI solutions that, as of today, don't really exist beyond our movie screens or Sci-Fi novels.

Experts may shout me down at this statement, but until we see a commercially viable General or Super Intelligent solution, it's still not here in my opinion.

My advice: focus on the left while observing the right of this picture.

General AI

3) Theory of Mind

General AI is where a computer learns emotion and theory of mind. It will learn beliefs, read emotions, comprehend thoughts, and form opinions beyond a single task or known outcome.

It will start to mimic human emotion – and I stress *mimic* because it will still likely be reactive to response rather than self-aware.

→ Impacts on our lives

Some incredible progress is underway, and regardless of its true capability, the impression of truer intelligence will be a massive step forward and bring the possibilities of truly incredible solutions.

Imagine Scout taking an intervention outside of her programme. Maybe she hears that you are upset and intervenes off her own bat... or she blocks notes or messages based on a bias or opinion, or she considers it may cause possible offence.

Should this day arrive, companion solutions will have huge societal impacts, transforming societal interactions as emotion and empathy are provided Companions As A Service.

Let's remember the line of reality for now, and, as crazy as both General and Super Intelligence sound, let's not be too naïve. Remain aware of the progress already made in our time and consider what our ancestors would have thought if we had explained our lives of today to them.

History teaches us to rule nothing out. Who knows what progress the incredible minds of the current and future generations might achieve?

Super Intelligence

4) Self-Aware

Raised eyebrows in full effect! And I'm with you!

This is where AI becomes self-aware with its own consciousness and surpasses the intelligence of humans. A point described by many Futurists as the moment of singularity, with some suggesting we could actually reach this point in many of our lifetimes, as early as 2045.

Not a new prediction, and in 1972, MIT (Massachusetts Institute of Technology) predicted that this would lead to the eventual collapse of society by 2040.

Incredible claims and fast-approaching dates yet a topic that will continue to divide the most intelligent minds and eminent Scientists and Academics alike while we watch with interest and begin to see news headlines and Sci-Fi movie scripts blur.

→ **Impact on our lives**

Should we ever reach the point of true, self-aware AI, staying relevant will be the last of our worries. AI would hold the potential to completely remove work as we know it, and we would go on to do other things... what they are, I'm not quite sure and perhaps that's a sequel book.

• • •

Practical Robots

As with all technology developments, things tend to get better and cheaper as they progress over time – remember Moore's Law.
Robotics will undoubtedly follow the same pattern as we move Robots from niche use in manufacturing or industrial use cases (or simply for vacuuming our floors) into widely available mainstream solutions across broader industries to aid human roles.
As with AI, if it's predictable, repetitive, manual, or dangerous, the chances are a Robot will soon be doing it instead and better than a human ever could.
From Robots working on our behalf in dangerous environments, drones working at height, self-driving cars, and exoskeletons giving humans Robotic superpowers, there will be no shortage of practical use cases for Robots. They will take the 'labour' out of 'manual labour'.
And as Tesla looks to develop a humanoid Robot that promises to do our housework and DIY for just $20k, the day may come far quicker than we previously thought.

→ Impact on our lives

As with the introduction of many new innovations over history, they usually bring improvement to the lives of many for obvious and practical reasons. As with AI, Robotics are already replacing many people in roles and will cause significant disruption in the future.

They make better chess players than us, they are safer drivers, and again as with AI, they don't need sleep or a pension plan.

However, while the Robotics progress accelerates, it will be massively limited by regulation and concerns for safety, privacy, and disruption in the jobs market.

Robotics comes with massive possibilities, and we have to ask: could a Robot do *our* job?

Fighting this progress will be futile, just as it was for the Luddites in the 1800s. Working with Robots is the middle ground we should focus on.

CoBotics

Whether it's AI or Practical Robots taking over our duties and tasks, the reality of them taking over all our roles is unlikely.

Think about your own job; I'm sure AI will aid my role and life massively in the future, but well over 50% of what I do would need General or Super Intelligence to replicate, so I'm hopeful that the majority of us will stay relevant for many years to come.

So, working alongside AI and Robots is likely the outcome for many of us. This is known as CoBotics, where we focus on cooperative working to improve efficiency.

→ Impact on our lives

As AI and Robotics take on tasks, as explained in the Story of Scout, we will be able to reduce our working hours.

It will be interesting to see how society adapts to this trend.

Will we end up doing more work, or will we enjoy the time we get back? Only time will tell. Hopefully, we won't forget our recent history where we embraced tech to simply work harder, and this time, we will take and use the efficiencies for a more positive benefit to us.

Voice Assistants

As in the story of Scout, we are likely to use voice more in the future instead of our keyboards. This will be due to the growth of both Glass and more personalised AI solutions, with which voice is just easier than manually inputting a reply or question.

We will still use keypads on our phones for privacy when we are unable to speak our inputs.

→ Impact on our lives

Very simply, this will be the continued progression of our current Voice Assistants, who use AI to provide more proactive interactions through our daily lives.

As described in the story of Scout, our voice allows us to access information quicker and multitask more – all without the need to look at a screen or device. An aid to our current lives, as AI voice replaces the text notifications we receive today.

Then in time, we'll be accessing our own personalised version of Scout in the AI As A Service model, which will subconsciously start to make AI feel very real, despite it being a computer and will likely change our relationship with technology forever.

Think Space Odyssey's *'Open the pod bay doors, HAL.'*

Quantum Computing

Understanding quantum physics is a whole library of books in itself – and not one I'm qualified to write.

So, here are the basics we need to know to demystify this technology.

In brief, progression and advancement in computing over the last 200 years are now hitting a wall.

As with Moore's law, everything gets smaller and more powerful over time. However, with some computing components now approaching the size of an atom, the usual methods of development and working in bits and bytes have reached their limits.

So, Developers now turn to quantum properties, where instead of working in 0's and 1's, quantum allows us to work in parts of either and multiple combinations of both, something called 'super positions', to build far superior computers that work at exponential speeds.

This is likely to provide the power source for the future of AI systems, as well as improve outcomes in more niche areas such as advanced cyber security, financial modelling, and medical research and drug development.

It's unclear whether the reality of a home PC powered by quantum will ever appear, but who knows how this field may progress.

→ **Impact on our lives**

Quantum, coupled with developments in AI, will bring a range of benefits to us via advances to health and science that would have previously taken many more years. At a personal technology level, we are unlikely to see the impact of this technology for some years to come.

High-speed Connectivity

The future will be fast, and so too will the connectivity.

The majority of the solutions mentioned here will require super-fast connectivity to deliver them and make them usable and useful in our lives.

This will see a continuous roll-out of increasingly fast networks. 5G, and soon-to-follow 6G, technologies will give the impression of wire-free networks.

5G will connect the mass voice of IoT devices, using increased speeds to make our experiences in XR and the Metaverse instant to the point we will be able to read emotion in a video call; it will bring almost zero latency (when data is processed so fast there is practically no delay), so we don't talk over each other.

Providers will mesh their fixed and mobile networks together to provide a ubiquitous and seamless connectivity experience for us.

Public Wi-Fi networks will largely disappear as faster mobile solutions surpass them in performance and security. Satellite solutions will provide overlay networks for hard-to-reach locations or areas of low investment.

We won't really care how it gets to us, but we will consider it a life service as more aspects of our lives become connected.

→ **Impact on our lives**

Impressive as our networks are today, considering the landmass we have to cover and the demand for bandwidth, we will continue to see improvements in the performance of these networks and ultimately reach a point where high-speed access is everywhere.

When this happens, it will help further release us from locations completely. The tasks you currently save for an office or home location due to connectivity speeds will be everywhere, and we will see an end to 'wires' as 5G and 6G solutions bring true ubiquitous coverage.

3D Printing

Far from new technology, many people now own home 3D printing machines, allowing us to print a range of items but usually basic items for a project or items simply for novelty or just for fun.

The Internet holds a template for pretty much anything you can think of, but the reality is that many printers are gathering dust due to the lack of need or complexity of making them work reliably.

Its truer opportunity is more in industry, where specialist 3D printers can print everything from a complete house through to a spare part for a machine on site. This rapid replacement and on-location manufacturing is already bringing incredible efficiencies to many industries and will fuel major growth across sectors in the future.

It will also massively reduce carbon in the supply chain and, in time, greatly reduce dependencies on and delays in imports.

→ **Impact on our lives**

Affordable home units will continue to improve in quality and reliability but also expect to see Printing As A Service, where local print shops will appear, and you can simply message them a template of what you want to be printed, and they will print it for you using their industrial grade high-quality printers.

Industrial printing will create new jobs and evolve many existing jobs, as the technology continues to improve.

So, this is just a sample of some of the incredible technologies that are either already quickly developing or rapidly appearing on the horizon.

In many situations, these technologies will either replace us or complement what we do. We need to be aware of these and learn a little more about them.

I will continue to share more information and developments on these and other technologies in some short videos available on the Future Of Us website. www.futureofus.co.uk

• • •

Collision of Technology

While progress in these specific technologies is considered in terms of what we know from what's available today – or the progress and developments currently underway – we also need to consider the power of some of these technologies when they are combined and used together.

Some amazing innovations don't always fly the first time.

If you think about the solutions you use in your digital lives today, many of these rely on another key innovation, and together, they bring amazing solutions and possibilities.

Imagine your mobile device without a high-speed data network to power it. The iPod and mobile Internet collided to bring us the iPhone.

The electric car was invented way back in 1832 by Robert Anderson, but this remained simply a concept until Tesla progressed battery technologies to make it a viable solution some 176 years later.

Zoom and Teams are not new technologies but imagine them without high-speed broadband or mobile networks – or even without the pandemic to force us to use them every day!

These are just a few examples of technology collisions that have already brought some amazing solutions to life.

This pattern will continue into some of the new technologies I covered earlier, such as the growth of connected things in our IoT towns and cities, interacting with new XR Glass-type solutions, high-speed 5G networks (which will bring locations digitally to life), and Artificial Intelligence solutions, which will interoperate with us at every step of our physical or virtual journeys.

As new technologies continue to emerge, the opportunity for more collisions grows and holds promise not only for some exciting and interesting solutions but for rapid transformation.

The potential is massive; the opportunities will be embraced by Innovators, and we are likely to see some incredible solutions drive further change, acceleration, and transformation in our time.

• • •

Societal Transformation

While these rapid developments and continuous progress will bring significant transformation to our lives, however impressive they are, they will not be the only drivers.

The choices we make as a society around how we use these technologies, what we do for a living, and who we work for will be the most powerful drivers for our future.

*'If **Technology** is the vehicle for change,*
*and **Innovation** is the fuel,*
***Society** is the driver.'*

Throughout history, the balance of power has usually sat with the employer. Organisations provided the systems of industry and commerce, which required a workforce of labour and intelligent minds to run these in return for wages, stability, and a degree of certainty.

Employers gradually improved conditions and wages over time, and the majority of generations fell into a familiar pattern of work and leisure.

The nine to five; using the weekend to catch up with family or friends, read the paper, take windy walks, and have a glass or two of wine.

Sounds familiar, right?

For the majority of us, this is 'our normal'. It's a pattern passed down from the generation before us and our expectation of the generation in front.

But is it right?

A number of key factors in play will, and are already, challenging our norms as we begin to see different ways of working and living. There are changing priorities across the board – driven either by new technologies or by new generations opening their eyes to very different expectations and preferences and what work and purpose mean to them.

In response, we hear stories of entitled Millennials or lazy Generation-Zs driven by a lack of staff in our stores and restaurants or because they challenge the old traditions such as 'first in the office and last to leave', and the 'always on' culture as devices make us available anytime.

I disagree; I call these people the Innovators of our time. The new generations that will show us a new way to live and work, often using technology as the enabler.

And ultimately, who set our pattern of work and who decided this was the way it should always be? If we look back to history, we don't dream of working twelve-hour shifts six days a week and find it difficult to believe our ancestors did so.

The same thing is happening now.

Once again and to stress my point, we will go down in history as teachers of the future tell children about how we used to wake early, cram ourselves onto trains and motorways, sit in offices from nine to five (mainly to email the person sitting next to us), return home late, sit looking at emails on our device all evening and then repeat five days a week, as our children of the future will simply ask... '*Why?*'

We will, of course, defend our position with the need to access computers and networks prior to the days of cloud computing and super-fast home broadband. But now that the technology is here have our understandings and attitudes followed suit?

We've been a little naïve to the reality of our time.

The nine to five model has been in place for nearly a hundred years. Yet now, through a mixture of ambition and sometimes greed, our cultures moved us to work beyond the eight hour day and five day week, as our 'you can have it all culture', has led to some pretty challenging realities.

Health and well-being were sometimes knowingly and unknowingly overlooked by progress and profit. And while we sought and embraced equality of opportunity, we unconsciously slipped from a single household salary model to a need for two salaries becoming barely enough.

We farmed out the childcare of our children, average household debt soared, and retirement investments fell short of the generations before us.

I'll put the violin away for now as, let's be honest, despite these concerns the majority are doing ok and cannot really compare their lives to some of the tougher hardships of the past.

However, we should still challenge that this doesn't make it right to work the way we do today for what we get back in comparison. Burnout, stress, and unhealthy lifestyles are becoming the norm across a huge part of society – people often struggle to keep the wheels of their lives on track, muscling on to a short retirement if they make it.

Many of you will be nodding along at this point, thinking about a time the walls started to close in on you. I say: welcome, friends, you're in good company.

I remember the sobering moment, after another busy period at work and some very long hours, when I gently drifted off to sleep on the motorway on another 5 a.m. drive to our head office.

Thankfully, I worked out very quickly what the rumble strips at the edge of the motorway lanes are for; I jumped awake and vowed I needed to make a change for myself and the very young family still tucked up asleep at home.

Overall, I think we are ready for change. As we think about the precious little time we have to ourselves in our busy lives, it begs the question: are we really living?

> *The average retirement age is 66 years old*
> *The average life expectancy is 78 years old*
> *If you start working at 20 years old, you would have worked 45 years in return for 13 years of retirement*

I'm not suggesting we down tools – you wouldn't listen if I did anyway; you're not reading this book because you're happy to plod along – you want more, and I'm with you.

What I'm suggesting is that we use our incredible technology, coupled with our experience of the past and changing attitudes of today and some of the guidance in books such as this to work smarter, not harder. I'll touch on this in more detail later in the book.

Technology has allowed us to work in different ways during Covid, and it's improving all the time. It's making us super-efficient and holds the promise of improving our lives further in the future. It's time to embrace it and take back control of our lives... **it's time to start living.**

Generational Drivers

So, who's right? Who should lead the revolution? We have four generations in the workforce today, all with different ideals, views, and preferences.

How do we navigate the future together and learn from each other?

Of course, we all think we're right, naturally, based on our experiences in our education and careers to date, which can widely differ across people.

Age and experience may not be the best skills to manage the volatility of a fast-paced future, but energy and new ways may lead to rushed decisions that time will not allow us to reverse. Working together as a collective will be essential to drive rapid change and ensure there's a smooth ride ahead.

So let's take a quick look at the generational teams making up the workforce of today...

Baby Boomers

The high birth rates after WW2 provided both the name and the huge workforce supporting growing the industries post-war.

They used their collective might to gain majority votes on the societal and industrial issues important to them, a pattern that still continues to this day. The majority of Boomers are now into retirement, but a good number are still in the workforce where they generally occupy senior positions in organisations or on boards and are seen by many as the voices and guides of experience as they pass the baton to Generation X.

Meanwhile, they head into largely comfortable retirements, supported by long tenures in a small number of firms, final salary pensions, property ownership, and investment wealth.

Many boomers have adapted to technology and innovation in a bid to stay relevant, but this is still largely considered a younger-generation skillset or something requiring dedicated learning and expertise.

Boomers are traditional in their communication, largely preferring face-to-face or telephone call interactions.

Generation X

The MTV generation or bridge generation who followed the patterns of work set by the boomers before them, fuelled by high ambition and encouraging entrepreneurialism in an era of economic growth, thereby bridging the wealth divide.

They have a strong focus on status and are driven by the 'you can have it all' attitude pushed by movies and Yuppies.

Technology and innovation appeared late in their school years, as computers began to appear in schools and family homes. The boom of satellite TV made the world a smaller place and opened a world of entertainment and possibility.

The generation that is most guilty of overworking competed for jobs in times of high unemployment and industrial disruption. They are digital immigrants with varying attitudes to tech, from early adopters to avoiders.

These are the text generation – preferring to message each other or communicate face to face if time allows in their work schedules.

Millennials

The sophisticated set of challengers.

The first generation of Digital Natives growing up with rapidly advancing technologies and understanding their power. They're using their awareness to challenge the status quo and bring new expectations for both the brands they interact with and the employers they work for.

Immune to traditional sales and marketing models, they have less loyalty to brands and use the power of technology to shop in different ways.

Their sharing societies form new communities of engagement, learning and interaction.

Living life to the full, they explore the world and delay the traditions of careers, marriage, and families, extending their educations and living with parents longer.

Now a core and confident part of the workforce, with a strong focus on technology and innovation as they take new perspectives into the boardroom of both new and long-standing firms alike.

They prefer to interact over multiple social platforms, saving face-to-face for networking and career progression.

Generation Z

'Generation sensible' and the true children of the Digital Revolution, they were born with advanced technology, living and communicating in a new world. Strongly focused on social issues, they drink less and are cautious about taking risks.

Growing up with a Life As A Service model, they will be less likely to opt for ownership commitments and prefer the flexibility of rental and pay-as-you-use services.

With less loyalty to brands and employers and preferring flexibility and choice, they will have less generational wealth transfer and high living costs.

They will diversify their income and use the Gig Economy model to work for multiple organisations while continually evolving their learning.

More comfortable with online interaction than physical, they establish smaller online friendship groups and immerse themselves in virtual environments.

Generation Alpha

A generation yet to find its tags or form its own habits but with suggestions of the Screen Age who are likely to live and work in a world of technology that we might struggle to comprehend today.

Their pursuits of knowledge are never-ending, and they hold continuous learning in equal measure with work.

They will experience and be comfortable working alongside both Robots and people and will enjoy far more 'them' time as they bring a balance to their lives we will envy in our old age.

They will swap handsets and screens for Glass and AI Voice Assistants and be present in both digital and virtual worlds.

Combined this rare merging of both collective experiences and new attitudes in both the workforce and wider society will bring significant and positive growth as each generation learns from and influences the others.

It won't always be a walk in the park, but the voice of experience and diverse knowledge – coupled with the power of youth and fresh attitudes to work – will lead to probably the fastest acceleration of transformation ahead.

Now let's take a look at some of the other driving factors of change in play today

The Covid Accelerator

While change and progress is constant and expected. The Covid pandemic was a key accelerator of adaption across the generations.

Progressions in technology meant we could work and shop remotely as the pandemic closed our offices and high streets. Lockdowns proved the technology worked, and we worked in new ways to keep our lives and businesses running.

We used technology to be super-efficient as the lack of travel gave us time back to spend with family or to focus on our overall health and well-being. We had time to take stock of many things, including what we did for a living and who we did it for.

The Great Resignation kicked in, and people began to consider their lifestyles and family preferences over the wants of their companies or their own personal career ambitions. The impacts of Covid brought transformation that would have otherwise taken ten to twenty years to realise.

While the stats of Covid's impact vary widely, for many, the impacts (while significant to date) haven't been fully realised as of yet.

We're still some way off a model of consistency or a semblance of normality on many fronts. Politicians and business leaders appeal or demand a full return to the office in a bid to rebalance the economy or model they know worked so well for them previously – but people are still making their choices, and, while labour is scarce, the people are in the driving seat on this one.

They are dictating their wants and needs, what they will do, and most importantly, where they will do it from as people sit on video calls from home in shorts and t-shirts in the company of their exercise bikes and lockdown puppies. I will cover this in more detail in Chapter 6.

> *'The past is behind, learn from it. The future is ahead, prepare for it. The present is here, live it.'*
> **Thomas S. Monson**

Environmental Responsibility

Another key factor of our societal evolution and the current time is the impacts progress has had, and continues to have, on the environment.

While the Industrial Revolution has driven the progress of today, it's been at a great cost to our planet. We've done more damage in the last 250 years than the previous 4.5 billion years before it.

The outputs of our progress generate mass pollution and accelerate global warming, often with little awareness, followed by little regard, of its true impacts on our planet.

Growing awareness driven by Scientists, Activists, and passionate campaigners is pushing this high on society's agenda, both influencing our own personal decisions and helping to drive higher government action globally.

World leaders must unite on the agenda and instigate their own local regulations and rules for change.

But let's be clear: policies and mandates for change in industry will not be delivered by regulation alone, and it will need more than Greta Thunberg frowning on a news feed to deliver the change required.

Everybody needs to place the environment at the heart of their key decisions. We'll consider how green the suppliers of our services are, the carbon policies of the companies we work for, and our own choices – from the cars we drive to the journeys we make to our power usage.

The pandemic helped the environmental focus massively.

While we closed our offices, airports, and high streets, our planet enjoyed the biggest reduction in carbon its ever seen, greater than any previous economic crisis or even periods of war.

The question now is whether we will knowingly return to old habits and patterns of travel without considering our environment. In honesty (and reality), I think we will see some genuine consideration, but it will also be used as part of a wider argument as we negotiate the future of our working patterns and practices, and we ask whether it's really acceptable to travel every day when the majority of us no longer really need to.

As with any campaign of passion and purpose, the green agenda will be led by inspirational leaders, public figures, and a cast of celebrities calling for our attention and action to support the cause.

This will not only drive change but will keep it high on the newsreels and will crucially influence younger generations to ensure their future 'normals' have the environment at the heart of their focus.

They will come to the world as employees and consumers with higher expectations of their suppliers and employers alike. They will drive the environment into fashion and subtly change current societal trends from the 'follow me around the globe' posts on Instagram to posts of more consideration for the local great outdoors and wild hiking, cycling, and swimming themes.

As industry initially polluted the planet, it is also now playing a key role in reversing the impacts.

Organisations must set out their responses to both regulations and our expectations, publishing bold and aggressive carbon targets and significantly changed internal policies.

The combination of regulations and societal pressure quickly made ESG (Environment, Social, and Governance) policies a major focus for every organisation, as they either look to prove to customers that they were sustainable organisations or as a tool to attract the best talent to their organisations.

Regardless of their true drivers or intentions, we'll take it!

This focus is having a positive knock-on impact as they set high benchmarks for their suppliers and the organisations they work with, providing positive action in areas of industry that may not deal directly with customers. We pass on our expectations to them via the wider supply chain.

This environmental focus and the changing societal attitudes to work are bringing positive drivers for real change. Long may it continue.

Progressions in technology will play a significant role in this. Remote working tools in both the office and the field will force improvements as technology allows more people to truly travel without moving.

Again, while the Industrial Revolution may have been initially responsible for polluting our planet, the Digital Revolution, and the Future Of Us as a society will be the saviours who reverse this.

I'm confident we will make the right choices.

Business of Disruption

If we consider the current collisions, the majority have been spotted and delivered by a handful of smart Entrepreneurs or very innovation-focused organisations.

But one key driving factor that will likely drive even faster change is the growing business of disruption. This is not a new sector or industry, but instead a realisation that businesses need to evolve at a far greater pace as they compete for customers.

Staying still and doing what they've always done is no longer an option for any organisation – super tech-savvy customers now expect more from their favourite brands.

We want new digitally interactive services, we want to self-serve via apps, and ultimately, we want our brands and suppliers to predict our needs and either solve issues before they happen or make great recommendations to us proactively.

'Innovation over invention.'

And if we consider the task at hand, while organisations consider the big, game-changing inventions, true inventions are far rarer and few and far between.

Therefore, they instead focus their efforts on innovation over invention, deploying dedicated teams to look for marginal improvement and problems to solve that will make their business more efficient and appealing.

They will put the challenge out to the workforce and also use gamification and the Gig Economy to seek wider innovations.

I'll touch on this in more detail in the Future Of Work chapter later.

I speak on this point from the very close experience my day job allows me, as pre-pandemic, it was difficult to have a conversation with a board member about innovation.

It was often seen as 'nice to do' if time allowed, or we'd see a sceptically raised eyebrow at the reality of some of the new technologies under review.

Yet the door is now wide open, and a growing number of organisations are actively looking to work with partners, suppliers, Innovators and Futurists in a bid to stay relevant and drive their own Digital Transformation agendas. Innovation now moves from the nice to do to something that needs to be done as part of the reality and necessity of change.

And in turn, this will result in a wave of progression of goods and services that will land with us as customers.

The other driving factor in the business of disruption is, of course, profit.

How else can businesses change or transform their offerings and bring new solutions to drive further profits, find new customers, and capture our digital spend?

A pattern of 'Everything As A Service' is also appearing as providers move from up-front costs to monthly fees and pay-as-you-go and -use models. This helps affordability for customers, as it gives us instant, low-cost access and also helps organisations increase recurring revenues and open new markets.

Additionally, it drives greater investment into start-ups as revenues from these models are easier to track and provide a faster generation of cash. I expand on this in Chapter 7.

This move will see all organisations place a significantly higher focus on innovation as it moves far higher up their boardroom agendas.

This will see a very volatile landscape form across industries, and for us, a rapid and continuous stream of great solutions and evolving services.

There May Be Trouble Ahead

But this need and focus must be carefully balanced in organisations as it is likely to bring a volatile landscape across many industries, not only in those we trade with but also who we work for.

For many organisations, while the subscription model might be the answer to increasing profits, it will also bring uncertainty and risk.

The competition for our attention coupled with the increased cost of living means that while building an annuity model is a great idea, it might be counterproductive, as people are now carefully evaluating their outgoings with considerations to the wider increasing costs of living.

Solutions with a recurring cost will have to be brilliant, truly brilliant, for us to justify and continue the monthly payments.

Innovation that doesn't solve a problem is a gadget, and we won't be able to afford the luxury of gadgets.

Organisations without strong enough or continuous improvement plans will struggle to stay relevant and defend against new entrants, or wider competition, for our increasingly pressurised digital spend.

Another factor will be the organisations that don't evolve quickly enough – those that continue to do what they've always done and miss the societal evolution and changing expectations.

It's not always about being first.

Apple didn't invent the smartphone but instead used hundreds of innovations to dominate the market before evolving the revenue model by using the device alongside access to services such as applications, storage, and music.

And at an industry level, we saw innovation's disruption in retail as many organisations either didn't fully appreciate the trends and level of transformations underway or were unable to evolve their traditional businesses to respond quickly enough.

It takes the average organisation 320 days to launch/evolve a product or service.

That's a lifetime in our fast-paced digital world, and companies who can't adapt their businesses to respond far quicker will be disintermediated by more agile organisations or start-ups and pay the ultimate price.

This is not a prediction; it's already happening all around us. We will and do vote with our feet.

Everyone's an Entrepreneur

Back in the early days of computing, the cost of access to technology and services needed to launch a website, online business, or application could quickly run into tens of thousands of pounds, meaning only current firms with funds in place or well-backed start-ups could be present in the digital world.

Now, with Moore's Law and competitive innovations, we could build a website with online payments and launch it in the time it takes you to read this chapter and for about the same price as this book.

the future of us

This access to computing power, cloud storage, and services has massively opened up the world of commerce and innovation to anyone with a good idea or commercial ambition.

Everyone's a business, and while many won't succeed, this vast field of triers will likely generate far more of the sorts of genius innovations we didn't know we couldn't live without.

We also have a wider sharing economy ecosystem of Developers making their code widely available to others as open source, encouraging people to use this to further develop ideas in the name of progress and for the greater good.

These factors combined will bring impactful change and rapidly increase the adoption and evolution of technology. Be it machines doing more of our jobs, businesses competing for our digital spend, or them simply trying to stay relevant themselves – as digital evolution touches every single industry, it really will be survival of the fitness for the organisations we work with and for.

Summary

So, there's no crystal ball for the future. Some of the technology predictions here will fly, and others will fall, but if we consider these collective drivers for change, these will naturally complement one another and provide the ingredients for potentially rapid transformation.

We are in for an incredible journey ahead as we ride our very own wave of the Cycle of Innovation – we better learn to surf and fast!

'The Future will only have one speed: faster!
If you can't keep up, you'd better get fit.'
Jim Carroll – Futurist

Take Aways & Points to Consider

- What do you know about the Mega Trends and how are they impacting the industry you work in? We'll take a closer look at this in Chapter 8.

- What is the company you work for doing about these trends? Do they share their findings? Can you help them?

- We cannot expect Governments or our organisations to predict future transformation and to adapt to or survive the impacts. We will have to make our own preparations for this one.

- What is the carbon commitment and plans of the organisation you work for? And how do you personally positively impact them?

'We're not technical, right?'

4
understanding it all

'Where your fear is, there your task is.'
Carl Jung

understanding it all

So, the world is changing. We get it. We've already made some incredible progress, and as we look around, we can now begin to see and feel the true scale of the transformation in motion.

But our stage of the revolution will not only be fuelled by the constant advent of new technologies but also by emerging attitudes towards how we use these new technologies in our daily lives. But are we all on the same page? Do we fully understand it all? Is it all starting to feel a bit busy, a bit technical, and a bit confusing?

If so, that leaves us asking whether we can just leave it to the techies. Or whether we can kinda just hope we'll get by without too much disruption in our careers and lifetimes.

Well, hope is not a great strategy. But never mind – you received your 'Digital Future Guidebook' in the post, right? ... No, me either. We are about to navigate a period of transformation with a scale and pace unlike any other time in history. Yet we have no map, no guide, no teacher, and no leadership, leaving us to ask how we are supposed to understand it all.

Welcome, friend. Once again you're in good company. Unfortunately, there's no guidebook for this one, and yes, the pace of change is already outstripping our education systems, our Governments' transformation plans and policies, and the business models of many of the organisations we work for.

Very few will employ Futurists and, even if they do, even *we* don't have a crystal ball. Ultimately, we are all in the same position.

We are paddling out into the surf, seeing the waves of change swell in the distance, and preparing ourselves for the ride, all while history reminds us that it's not the first wave; it's simply *our* wave.

The reality is: it's really up to us to learn to surf fast and ride the wave of change together.

The future needs us!
Your future needs YOU!

But I'm Not Technical!

One of the biggest challenges we will face in the Future Of Us... is us! Our desire and ability to change will be just as big a challenge as trying to understand the plethora of new solutions entering our lives.

And with good reason, too! Anything that impacts or changes our jobs or livelihoods is always going to be met with natural resistance.

As the Dali Lama said: *The key to happiness is routine.*

And, regardless of your role or industry, you will likely have found a rhythm, routine, a pattern to your daily working life, that works for you.

Yet here comes a tsunami of new and confusing technologies, many set to change and mess up your routines without warning, and with little regard for our opinions and preferences. But what can we do about it?

We're not technical, right?

This is a statement I've heard hundreds of times in digital workshops and innovation sessions with my customers over the years, and a true one, but also, thankfully, a largely irrelevant one. The reality is that we don't need to be technical to survive the digital future; in fact, it's actually great that we aren't.

Sure, we will need lots of technical experts to design and build the technologies of the future – and I will take nothing away from the brilliant minds able to design and build the incredible technologies of today and tomorrow.

But we will also need lots of creative minds, as well as organised and logical thinkers, business leaders, and people just like you, to develop, manage, and run our businesses and governments of tomorrow.

We will all play a role; it's not about joining a technical knowledge contest to survive. It's more about a collective teaming of roles and minds, working together to constantly consider the 'how', and to be the voice that asks the 'why's' as we explore and build the future together.

It's Only Natural; It's Chemical

So, why do we resist change and push the 'I'm not technical' button so quickly? First, let's start with the science bit.

A small section of our brain called the amygdala is a complex structure of cells nestled in the middle of the brain, adjacent to the hippocampus – which is associated with memory formation. The amygdala is primarily involved in the processing of emotions and memories associated with fear, fight, and flight.

When the amygdala senses danger, it signals the release of stress hormones, preparing your body to either fight for survival or flee to safety, without any initiative from you. It just happens.

This chemical reaction is what has kept us alive as the human race, be it fleeing from predators as a prehistoric man, or adapting to new ways to hunt, live, and then work through the Industrial Revolution.

It's essential to keeping us on the ball and alive.

Anyone who's changed jobs, watched a child ride a bike without stabilisers for the first time, or been through a merger or redundancy process will know these precise feelings.

Those times when you are not in control of certain aspects and the fear, fight, and flight emotions all jockey for position in your brain. You are out of control, yet you must manage your emotions into submission.

And while we can't stop it, we can learn to manage it and be better prepared. This way, when change arises in the future, we can acknowledge it quickly, and then prepare and plan to manage these emotions in advance. For those who master this, the reality is that there is a great opportunity ahead in the Future Of Work. I will expand on this in the next chapter.

I also appreciate that it's not as simple as me saying, 'change is coming; get on with it'. Change can have some very challenging impacts on us mentally, and, for the majority of us, it's never easy to adapt.

This is not a fault; it's nature.

Sure, we have the exceptions: the radical early adopters, Entrepreneurs, and Innovators. But these people are low in numbers, the majority of us sit somewhere between loving the stability of a fixed routine and embracing 'a little' disruption to keep things interesting.

Next, I want to take a look beyond the chemical reactions of change and talk more about our personal attitudes to change based on individual experiences.

Who Are We

Before we can understand how to stay relevant in our own futures, we need to know who we are and our ability and resistance to change as a starting point.

We are all different. We each have varying experiences and attitudes, meaning there isn't a one-size-fits-all guide to future change. But it's important that we acknowledge our own starting points before we consider how to manage change going forward.

Ultimately, we fall roughly into four key camps, and your experiences (and possibly the job you do and the company you keep) will determine where you sit and whether you have the ability to drift somewhere between different camps

Digital Natives
- Likely grew up with technology
- Comfortable with Digital Solutions and apps
- Uses social media constantly looks for the new
- Threads and chats your norm
- Online over in-person meet ups

Digital Immigrants
- Open to the possibilities of technology
- Healthy FOMO but not concerned -- it's all a bit fast
- Keen to learn more and to stay relevant but unsure if you're too late
- A voyeur of social media with one toe in
- Messaging and meet-ups are your thing

Digitial Resister
- Cautious and intelligent observer
- Traditional
- Bringing an important balanced view
- Avoids social media but a professional peeper on the QT
- Face-to-face or the phone for you

Digital Adopter
- Embracing new technologies
- Gadget collector
- Big phone brigade
- Pushing the 'Art Of The Possible'
- Asking the whys and the why nots
- Messaging, chat, calls or Face to face work for you

understanding it all

Digital Natives

You've grown up with technology and possess a naturally good foundation and understanding of technology as a result. You were likely connected digitally from a very young age and are comfortable with technology. While you may not be a technical engineer, you understand the basics of how many technologies and applications work at a basic level.

Naturally understanding the power of the digital world, you are an intuitive learner and are confident in your knowledge, knowing you have a world of information in the device in your hand.

You manage many different applications and ongoing chats and discussions with ease, be it in your work or social communications, with multiple projects, tasks, and conversations in play at any time.

You don't feel a need to rush to complete these and are happy to dip in and out as required.

Social media is a natural part of your life and social interactions, yet you have a considered approach to your online presence and are savvy to the risks and dangers of the online world.

You likely seek out your own people based on your interests, looking to the next new place to hang out as traditional digital platforms become crowded.

You seek the crowd's knowledge and opinion, seeing this as a filter for the Wild West of an Internet search and the lure of the corporate marketing machines.

Digital Immigrants

You likely grew up in the early days of personal computing, followed by the Internet, which you initially watched with a degree of interest but uncertainty, and which you then learnt to love as you spent more time online.

You fondly remember a time before mobile phones and are beginning to sound like your parents, telling of a time before all this technology (or is that just me?).

That said, you have embraced technology along the way in varying degrees, some with real aplomb, as you've marvelled at some of its capabilities and possibilities.

You're likely Generation X, so prefer to text or WhatsApp with face-to-face social interactions serving you best. You have a mixed view of social media, flipping from loving to hating it in equal measure as you learn how to best manage it, but either way, you're still there and still peeping at it to keep your FOMO (Fear of Missing Out) under control.

You are keen to learn more about the digital world overall but are unsure whether the window of opportunity for you to do so has closed.

You have a go-to person for all your more complex IT and digital needs – this person advises you as they were an early adopter and are 'a bit techie'. You consult this person before you buy a phone, TV, or laptop.

You google stuff – in fact, pretty much everything, really – as a starting point for your research and learnings on any topic.

You're already seeing a clear step change in the technology in your industry and impacts on your day job.

You're feeling slightly nervous of these impacts and are unsure of the steps you need to take to either stay relevant or keep up.

Digital Resistors

It's highly unlikely that you're reading this book. Or, if you are, you're doing so with a raised eyebrow, suspicious of the realities of some of the technologies we've covered.

Your view is that it all sounds great but is a bit far-fetched in reality. And ultimately, you might be right; there's no crystal ball and you'll have likely enjoyed a successful career without ever really having to understand too much about Digital Technology so far.

understanding it all

You will also likely have a strong view on certain aspects of the wider digital worlds, such as online bullying and cybercrime. You do have a good point here, noting that you will find no bigger fan of Digital Technology than myself, for all the good technology can bring, but your views and caution on this point provides a healthy balance and a reminder to us all that it's not all rosy in the digital garden.

Overall, you are sceptical of the increasing pace of change based on your own experiences with technology in the workplace and wider society. You're unsure whether everyone is yet on board and see this as the biggest limiter to progress.

You will be a patient observer and a fervent researcher, taking time to learn the options in some detail before making any decisions.

You will likely avoid interacting in social media, often on moral grounds, and far prefer a phone call, face-to-face engagements, or short text conversations. You likely see text conversations as written telephone calls, so stick with a single chat thread until it's complete.

Digital Adopters

Many of you will fall somewhere between the Natives and Immigrants camps, but with a healthy level of Resistor thrown in on certain points. I'll call this group the 'Drifting Digital Adopters.'

You sit with your feet in different camps, based on your age, depending on the topic, or what works for you at the time. You see the possibilities of Digital Technology and you embrace them with open interest and intrigue but hold a healthy resistance to some of the more 'out there' developments.

This is often due to being simply overcome by technology's complexities, to the point you don't even want to attempt an understanding (search 'what is quantum computing' to prove my point here – sorry in advance).

You will, however, know a lot about a specific field, your topic of interest, or your hobby, but you know you don't know it all, and run small, self-initiated projects to learn everything you can in areas that interest you or the things you feel are more relevant or likely to impact you.

Despite this, it's highly likely you didn't do amazingly well academically.

Why?

Because you're wired slightly different to the parameters of the education systems and your intrigue of the possibilities brings a natural impatience to your career journey. You challenge everything, but usually quietly, as you're interested more in satisfying your own thirst for knowledge than overstating your opinions and views to others.

You are the person the Digital Immigrants ask for help, as they class you as a 'bit techie', even though your own confidence in your own self-taught, Googled, and YouTubed digital skillset feels very different.

You have a million applications on your phone from the heaps of things you've tried out over the years. You will have voice assistants controlling your lights and music at home, have a number of different devices (such as laptops, tablets, and phones), and likely gave up paper in your day job many years ago.

You have a bigger phone than your friends and colleagues, and drawers full of old gadgets that didn't stand the test of time, along with a loft full of old consoles and a VR headset that you bought... purely for the kids, right...?

You bought SLR cameras back in the day and invested a little bit in cryptos, just in case.

You're happy communicating on multiple platforms, adapting to fit the audience you are engaging with at the time.

Overall, you look to technology with an open mind and interest, happy to explore and consider the positive and negative impacts. But you also have a slight raised eyebrow toward the likely impacts of Robotics and AI.

As you look at the very basic and older technologies your own company provides you at work, suggestions of AI and Robots seem a long way away.

• • •

Our Generations

Also, it's not always age-related. While it's natural that we might find younger generations in the Digital Native camp as they have grown up with technology, it's not exclusively the case. We have many early adopters from older generations who actively embrace and relish new technologies as they seek out the latest innovations from their TVs, PCs, smartphones, and Smart Homes.

Ultimately, it's about attitude to change and evolution, not generational trends or attributes.

You might work with a leader from a younger generation who brings new innovations to your previously unchanged workplace, and you're struggling to adjust or keep up. You may be that young leader, frustrated that not everyone can see the potential for change and the power of technology in the same way you do.

Or you may bring your own experience into question a little further and play something of a cautious referee between the camps.

As explored in the previous chapter, we have four generations in the workforce today, with a new one on its way. Each bringing their different experiences, habits, and expectations. We are all different, and it's vital we respect and learn from each other as we all aim to work as a team and find the best outcome for us all.

Regardless of where you sit, as we pause to consider the views of the different generations, coupled with the current progress and the pace of change already underway, it can lead us to feel a little out of our depth.

We may even be unsure of how we got to where we are today, or whether we fully understand the progress made so far without now having to understand and learn new things – it makes us feel like imposters.

Embrace the Imposter

Another factor limiting our understanding is the point that we are often not actually sure how we ended up where we are today.

Have you ever wondered how you got to where you are?

Do you ever wake up and think: 'I don't have the qualifications or experiences to do this or the education and qualifications of my peers'? Yet I'll also assume you're in a career or role that you're likely doing very well in, and others looking in from the outside probably have a very different opinion of your skills.

The reason for this is that, societally, we have been conditioned to feel that we must be fully educated before we step into a career or profession, with an exam grading seen as a scale of worth and, in turn, our confidence in our ability depending on these.

Yet, the reality is that a large number of professions in the world of work have no associated academic qualifications, so although many of us match ourselves based on the qualifications we think we need or via industry vocational qualifications where possible, lots of roles actually fall between these, leaving people unsure and often unconfident in their fit for the job.

We've also grown up following a system our whole lives that tells us we must learn in a certain way; that we must achieve a set of qualifications as a starting point.

Yet the second we leave the education system; we immediately stop learning. So, we take our qualifications – or lack of them – into the working world, where they often define us but don't necessarily provide a true gauge of our abilities.

We are often a little hung up on these, too, again as a societal indoctrination. Those with high academic qualifications have been told by the system that they're elite, and those without them are thinking, assuming or in some cases being told that they're inferior.

While we focus on our faults and self-doubts, we miss out on gaining a key skill we can't learn from the education system: evolution and the ability to change.

Taking nothing away from the education system or academia, but regardless of your academic achievements, you should be proud that you ended up in a role without a perfect fit of qualifications or experiences and that you've adapted and evolved your own learning and skills in jobs without a guidebook to show you the way.

You are no charlatan and now must turn any imposter doubts into focus. Rather than giving yourself a hard time about your perceived shortcomings, instead, invest this energy into learning more about your industry or a new skillset.

You have done this naturally already to get to where you are – and to even have these doubts in the first place. You need to continue doing this and not underestimate the value and power of adaptability. Your employers, and future employers, will be far more impressed by your industry knowledge, adaptability, and new learnings than your degrees and diplomas.

Understanding Our Change Journey

So, the chemical reaction is out of our hands, coupled with our psychological reactions and self-beliefs, and shaped by our life experiences and demographic attitudes. All of which form our starting point in understanding and managing change.

Now that we've 'boxed' ourselves into the Digital Camps/Types we either resonate with or feel slightly awkward inside, let's look at the Cycle of Change itself in a bid to better understand how we can manage the inevitable changes ahead – regardless of our neurological or demographic starting points.

As innovation comes in cycles, so too does change. (See **Managing Change** graph on next page) It takes us from the initial Shock, Disruption, Realisation, or Denial and often leaves us with a hope we can ignore it until it goes away.

This is closely followed by Frustrations as there are changes to our routine, and reality begins to kick in. We then enter the Acceptance and Experiment stage, where we look at how we can work with change before learning to integrate with things and get used to our new normal.

Think of your own experience with Covid and the waves of varying emotions caused by lockdowns: from the surprise of this unprecedented time in history to the gradual acceptance that things are unlikely to ever be the same again.

understanding it all

Managing Change

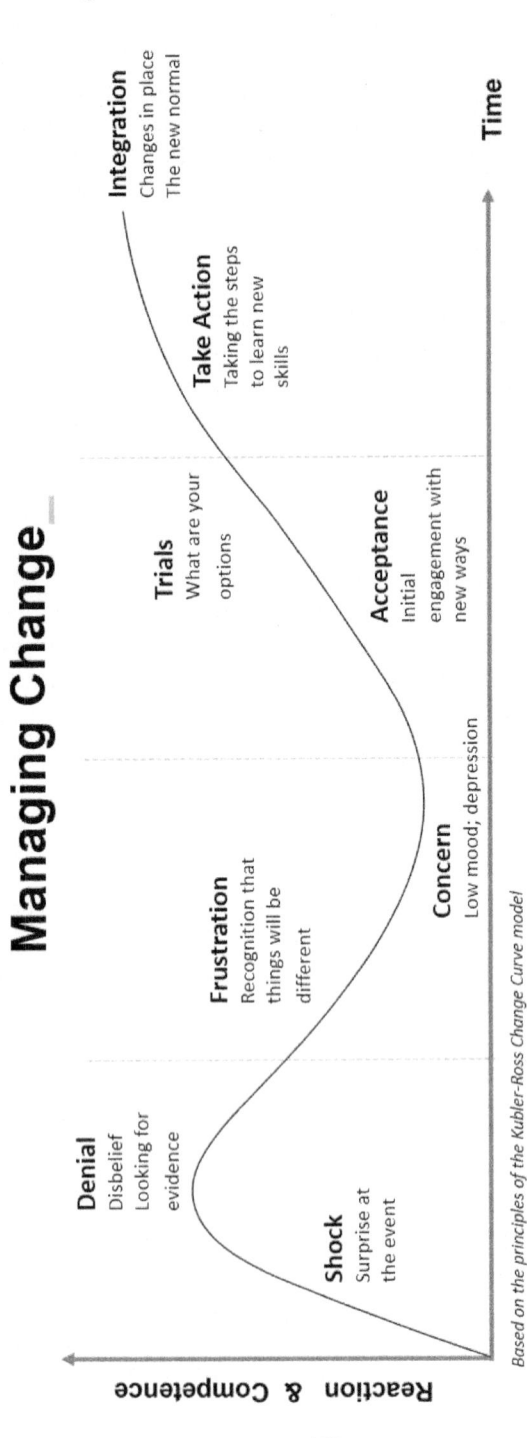

Shock — Surprise at the event

Denial — Disbelief Looking for evidence

Frustration — Recognition that things will be different

Concern — Low mood; depression

Trials — What are your options

Acceptance — Initial engagement with new ways

Take Action — Taking the steps to learn new skills

Integration — Changes in place The new normal

Reaction & Competence / *Time*

Based on the principles of the Kubler-Ross Change Curve model

All images are also available to view and download at www.futureofus.co.uk

Then move on to today's trials and experiments with hybrid working models, flexible locations and hours, and the ongoing headline-grabbing debates of what the office and city of the future will look like.

Understanding the process of change will help us massively reduce the shock and depression it can cause and will allow us to spend more time in the Experiment stage to understand how to work with change rather than trying to fight it.

When we know change is coming, tackling it head-on is the best, if not the only, option we have if we are to stay relevant.

And, more importantly, sane.

We should start the research when the Shock of change lands, if not sooner (I will expand on this in the next chapter). We need to consider what we know about the drivers of change. Is it technology or a societal or generational trend? And how do we learn more?

Replace the Shock and Frustration with insight and clarity. Work out whether it's for you! It's easy for us to say, 'pull up the big boy/girl pants and get on with it', but does it work for you overall?

Here, you need to define whether your focus and efforts should be to understand your relevance in the outcomes of change or whether it's just not for you and you need to focus on something new.

What we can't afford to do is dwell on what we can't control. This is where the Depression stage comes in and takes precious time away from the next critical stage: Experimentation.

Using the facts of your research and insights, figure out where your strengths and weaknesses are so you can promote and address these, respectively. How can your experience and skills – coupled with open thinking – help you increase your relevance?

understanding it all

Start to consider some of the changes you are currently experiencing in your role or industry. We will come back and start to map some of the changes in play later in this book and look at how we manage change, start our experimentations, and take steps to stay both better informed and relevant.

If you're unsure, reach out to colleagues, your boss, a mentor, or friends and family and take their views of changes in play and ask the 'why's' to qualify your understandings.

My point here is that we need to have an appreciation of the fact that new innovations and technologies will keep coming; we can't slow them down and learning to manage this wave of change in our Innovation Cycle is a far better strategy than fighting the inevitable tide.

I've used this technique throughout my career, and I've also seen some very non-technical people use it, too, to embrace change and turn it into brilliant success. Many of these people are now classed as experts and thought-leaders in their field – but they're not technical, right?

We need to hold the stages of this diagram ready in our minds so that when change does appear, we are better equipped to acknowledge and quickly switch our focus to embrace, take action, and seek out any possible opportunities. I will expand on this in the development tool sets at the back of the book with more detail on how to review and manage change in practice.

• • •

Open & Future Mind, the What Ifs

Many years ago, in the early days of mobile phones, a colleague of mine suggested I'd wasted my money in buying my very first mobile phone, insisting they wouldn't take off!

I attempted to defend my rather expensive purchase, but as I only knew two other people with a mobile phone at the time, I was slightly lame in my argument. However, I do remember my rather weak closing statement as I contemplated the anxiety of some serious buyer's remorse as I said, 'Yes, but imagine if everyone had one.' (This was my 'what if'.)

Well, history tells us the outcome of that debate and I share this story not to prove who was right and who was wrong, but to show that he had closed off his mind to the very concept itself. Conversely, my argument was my open-mindedness – which, in honesty, did feel weak at the time.

Shortly after that conversation, I went to work for a mobile phone company that I still work for some twenty-eight years later, and he went on to be one of the very last people I knew to own a mobile phone... but I would bet the tide finally got him, and I bet he has an awesome smartphone in his pocket today.

Also, this could have been a different technology, and he could have been right.

If we think back to all the technologies mentioned in the Story of Scout, would we have the confidence to say they will all be as big as our mobile phones?

Could you have foreseen the mobile phone or smartphone a few years earlier?

Or the growth of the Internet, or the cross-generational adoption of applications such as Facebook?

Maybe an electric car beating a Ferrari?

No. But they happened, right? And all of them came from slow and humble starting points but then went on to gain both industry and market-leading positions.

Keeping an open mind is critical and thinking of the possibilities of each will be essential in planning for the future. We must consider the 'what if' or 'imagine if' questions we should ask rather than feeling the need to become a technical expert in a field.

We must keep from simply suggesting things 'won't take off' without doing at least a little research.

> *'Education is not learning the facts. It's rather the training of the mind to think.'*
> **Albert Einstein**

My call-out here is that we will all play a role in the future as the Revolution continues to gather pace.

Unlike the mobile phone, which kinda made sense despite sceptics and doubters, in fields such as AI, we're likely to see some crazy ideas and suggestions of what technology can do in the Future Of Us.

Having an open mind to their possibilities while accepting and embracing the fact that you don't need to fully understand all the technical aspects will stand us all in good stead. It's simply about playing your role.

To this point, no matter how great an idea is or how in-demand a product is, it will still need us all to play a role in delivering and developing it.

As a proof point, in 2007, Apple created and launched probably the most 'in demand' product of our time. They also moved from 21,000 employees to 154,000 in order to manage the business and address the demand.

Yet, it's safe to say that the majority of that workforce couldn't even take the front off an iPhone, let alone build or programme it. Despite this, they collectively built one of the most successful products and businesses of our time and of all time, attracting the very best talent across the world.

As with the case of Apple, all businesses and industries will need a mass of logical thinkers, creative problem solvers, and adaptable employees who can understand enough to work with the technology as well as appreciate the importance of change in equal measure.

People who can look at how technology can make us, and our organisations, more efficient and effective. These will form some of the key and highly relevant skills employers will be looking for in the Future Of Us.

Summary

While you may feel out of sync with rapidly advancing technology, the future transformation will be about far more than just great Ideas.

The future will need wider expertise than the technology of hit innovations. Running a business in a high demand and limited-competition market is very different to running a firm in a highly competitive industry or saturated market.

We need your brains to drive the next stage of the Digital Revolution; we need wider skillsets and creative problem solvers with logical minds. We all work differently, and we will all play an important role.

Your skills and experience, coupled with an open mind, will bring with them experience and a different thought process essential to a business's survival and sustainability.

Greater understanding brings with it confidence.

Again, not to step into a technical knowledge contest, but let's consider the US Senators who challenged Mark Zuckerberg at the Senate hearing on the topic of data privacy and security.

The majority of them didn't even understand the basics of how Facebook's business worked, which isn't a complex model, really. Nor did they even understand how Facebook was able to provide one of the world's biggest applications completely free to 2.9 billion users. Leaving Mark Zuckerberg to point out, 'we sell ads'.

This is an incredible example of what we must all avoid.

The Senators entered into a government debate about **our** data, many with real attitudes and arrogant confidence, based on zero actual understanding of the basics. It's crazy to even consider that they were happy to lead the review without first investing time into a little research of the whats, hows, and whys.

We have an opportunity now to be the ones who do understand the basics and consider the possibilities with an open and balanced mind. We can be those who learn to adapt and manage change. This, alongside what we'll cover in the next chapters, will provide us with practical steps we can take to move us from simply understanding to staying relevant in the Future Of Us.

Take Aways & Points to Consider

- Accept that we don't need to know it all.
- Be comfortable with your natural skills; they're as important as the technical and incredible when combined with an open mind.
- Maintain that open mind in terms of the possibilities of technology, even the crazy stuff. Always consider the 'what ifs'.
- Know your starting point, who you are, and where you need to focus to manage the Cycle of Change.
- Again, give some thought to the changes already in play in your job or life. Can you clearly identify them? Or do you need to take a step back, or dig deeper, to better understand them? We will look closer at this in Chapter 8.
- Embrace your inner imposter and turn it into a force for good.

'Observing the future, for our future, has never been more important in the Future Of Us.'

5
the impact on our lives

'The future interests me – I'm going to spend the rest of my life there.'
Mark Twain

So, as a quick checkpoint and summary of what we've covered so far:

- We've looked at how the Story of Scout may change our lives in the future.

- We've acknowledged the considerable and incredible progress we've already seen in our lives and walked through the various drivers likely to accelerate the pace of our journeys ahead.

- We reviewed the process of change to understand our starting points and generational attitudes to change while agreeing that we don't all need to be 'technical' – while nature initially resists change, it also gives us the ability to adapt creatively as part of our natural evolution.

Now, before diving into the practical steps of staying relevant, I want to focus on two areas of significant importance to us all.

These areas will likely see considerable transformation and potentially disruptive impacts during our time. They will be driven by technology and societal transformation with the potential to transform our future economic landscape completely.

They are; How will we earn a living And, in turn, what is the *cost* of living in a digital future

I've pulled out these themes for special attention based on their importance to us and the fact they are mutually inclusive and careful advanced planning of these areas could bring considerable benefits to the Future Of Us and our children.

I will break these two elements down in more detail over the next two chapters. However, first I want to summarise my thoughts briefly and provide some initial rationale before fully articulating why I consider these areas the most important and possibly the most impactful in the Future Of Us.

The Future Of Work

On average, we spend a third of our lives asleep and a third at work, making what we do for a living a direct influence, if not a dictation, of how we spend the final third of our lives.

Overall, most of us followed the conventions of traditional work throughout our lives. Then came Covid, which totally transformed the way we live and work forever. Covid pushed an overnight adoption of technology that opened our eyes to new ways of working that we quickly embraced, allowing us to work in far more flexible ways.

As we reflect and experiment with different hybrid and flexible working models, we see technology as the enabler. However, our societal preferences and new attitudes towards work are the real drivers of lasting change.

Natural progressions in technology alongside the business opportunity presented by the potential to capture these changing trends will see a continuous wave of new technologies over the years ahead.

Organisations will work to balance the power and benefits of automation with a personal human touch to improve their services and solutions for their customers – for example, Robotics working alongside humans to complement our roles in small ways.

The potential of these efficiencies and new generational attitudes towards work will result in unavoidable changes ahead. We will work with Robots and AI as natural co-workers, meaning we will work far less and possibly for multiple organisations – either out of a financial need or desire and ambition for more.

As generations evolve from jobs for life and final salary pensions, and the life expectancy and relevance of the organisations we work for greatly reduce, the landscape of our careers will change.

This change will call for an end to the nine to five, the start of three- or four-day weeks, and the growth of Skills As A Service as the Gig Economy grows.

the impact on our lives

So, how do we prepare to work with these new technologies, learn new skills, and adapt to new working patterns to maintain and secure our incomes as we buck old traditions and attitudes and work less but smarter?

Life As A Service

While we consider how the Future Of Work may change how we earn our livings, are we also clear on how innovations and technologies may transform the economic landscape and, most importantly, our outgoings?

What do we need to earn, and what happens if the costs of our lives increase, but we have less financial stability and lack the ability to save for the future?

How will these trends shape a long-term transformation of economic landscapes and, in turn, our lives and the lives of the next generation? Who will pay for the future, and are we all aware of the building wave of economic change?

As the cost-of-living crisis deepens, with soaring fuel and utility costs, interest rate hikes driving up mortgages, and, in turn, rent, a national crisis needing Government intervention is in play. And while these points take the headlines, a very subtle but significant transformation is taking place behind the scenes and is already starting to hit our pockets.

This transformation is driven by the growing number of digital subscriptions leaving our bank accounts each month as providers move their commercial models from upfront purchase costs to subscription and rental options.

Businesses are either forced by investor preferences and a need to secure funding or driven by a requirement to entice sales in a growing cash-poor generation. If left unchecked, this transformational trend spells trouble way beyond the increased outgoings, which we currently link to fluctuations in inflation and increasing fuel prices and general cost of living rises.

It will lead to a long-term and more permanent transformation of the economic model for millions. Such a transformation will move us to a time of what I'm calling 'Life As A Service', where we own very little, invest very little and instead hire and rent both essentials and desirables items and services in our lives, for the convenience and instancy of ownership that these new models will bring.

My call-out here is that while we can't fight the tide of change, we certainly need to learn how to swim before we get out of our depths.

These trends will also create far deeper challenges across society.

While we may work less, we will very likely need to work far further into our lives. Additionally, costs will likely increase at pace, significantly impacting those most in need in our society, and accelerate the already significant Digital Divide and digital exclusion.

Summary

Collectively, how we earn a living and the cost of our lives have always been mutually inclusive, and this will never be more relevant in our time ahead. Our knowledge, focus, and relevance in these areas will increase in importance and be essential if we are to adapt and influence our journeys into the future.

So now, let's explore both points in more detail as we consider what we need to know and what's relevant as we plan our next stages in the Future Of Us.

'You're on mute.'

6
the future of work

'The future of work is really about people deciding to live and work in the way that they want.'
Stacy Brown-Philpot

New workplace technologies and changing societal attitudes towards work will likely bring the biggest and most significant transformation to our lives ahead.

As I said, the majority of us spend a third of our lives at work, some much more, and we've largely followed an unchanged pattern and attitudes towards work for the last 100 years. Each generation has learned from the last as they pass down the baton of the 'ways of work'.

Yet now, as we have explored in the 'pace of change' sections, new technologies and the Covid pandemic delivered an opportunity that proved we can make changes.

Not only this, but younger generations have brought new approaches and attitudes to work of the future. These have instigated a change and transformation that will become a historical moment of note.

In this chapter, I will explore several key components that will likely bring significant change to the Future Of Work. Starting with the advances and progresses in technology and then looking at the associated societal transformational impacts they will bring.

Technology

Continuous technological innovation and progressions will naturally bring new solutions, capabilities, and processes to the world of work.

Some of the solutions will make obvious sense. We will immediately see their relevance to aiding our daily lives and instantly adopt them. Others will potentially bring mind-blowing solutions and will hold the opportunity, concern, or promise to completely transform both our roles and industries alike.

Predicting these is sometimes obvious and easy; understanding more complex technologies can be challenging and overwhelming, meaning we distance ourselves from giving them the consideration and degree of due diligence we perhaps should.

As mentioned in the 'Understanding it All' chapter, we don't need to know everything about these technologies. We just need a high-level awareness of their make-up and capabilities.

This greater awareness allows us to decide for ourselves what's worthy of consideration or closer review and what's simply a clever gadget that is unlikely to transform our lives.

'Innovation that doesn't solve a problem is a Gadget.'

Solutions We Use

Can we imagine what would have happened during lockdown if we hadn't had Teams, Zoom, FaceTime, and WhatsApp?

How would we have managed to stay connected and keep our businesses going?

Sure, we had our phones and email, but the ability to see each other and share screens changed how we communicate forever.

The addition of seeing an image of us over just hearing a voice is the point of note here, and whether we are camera on or off. The option to see each other virtually provided us with the psychological connection we missed using phone calls and was the common-sense alternative to a physical meeting; this addition of using video is the key reason these solutions will transform the Future Of Work forever.

While these were not new solutions, providers made immediate improvements early into the pandemic, offering more features, such as whiteboards, dictation, recording, transcription, and time warnings.

The development of these solutions will continue and bring a collision of wider technologies and more useful features into play that will likely further transform our lives in the Future Of Work.

This change will also likely see more focused development as technology providers look to capture the rapidly expanding remote working market.

Now let's take a look at how these solutions and some of the mega-trend technologies I explained in Chapter 3 will evolve the solutions we use every day to do our jobs.

Then in Chapter 8, we'll look at how we can research and learn more about the impacts on our specific industries and roles and where we need to focus our learnings on staying relevant and informed.

Future of Communications and Tech

So, how might the mega-trends progress, improve from here, and transform the Future Of Work? As we explored earlier, technologies such as VR are already offering more immersive meeting solutions, and fuller immersion is a clear benefit as it removes those natural distractions of our phones and email.

Therefore, if you want a fully-engaged audience, VR is a great option. As the price of VR headsets comes down and solutions improve, I'm sure we'll see organisations use VR to break up the monotony of our back-to-back video call days or to ensure we're paying our full attention in training courses or to important company updates.

Our organisations will also build virtual versions of their sites to cater for remote engagements and to bring more uniformity to our remote and hybrid collaborations.

While it's great to see a bookcase or artwork in the backdrop of our colleague's home on a video call, people naturally feel slightly uncomfortable seeing a bed in the background, made or otherwise. Branded backdrops or predefined uniformed seats in a virtual environment would bring a more corporate feel.

AR, as described in the Story of Scout, may take some years to replace our screens. However, the interaction with our screens will provide what 3D TVs failed to do. Along with AR, there will be a realistic possibility to make our video callers pop out from our screens and provide us with a richer experience.

A virtual version of you will soon be available in the form of your customised avatar. Far from realistic or convincing for some time ahead, but avatars will grow in availability, and we will use them where we're unable to present ourselves remotely – for example, when travelling or working from a third location such as a coffee shop or shared location.

The topic of whether Robots will take our jobs is never far from the headlines. While our opinions may vary on the realities and timelines, AI is already currently, albeit quietly, delivering some incredible solutions and starting to take on tasks and duties.

We have yet to see solutions like Scout appear in our lives, but the clues to its development and adoption are already appearing in solutions such as Microsoft Viva, where AI proactively suggests tasks and duties at the start of our day.

This will continue, and solutions like this will take on more and more of our predictable and repeatable daily tasks. They will also move out of their native applications, and we will start to see industry AI As A Service solutions appear.

Think about your current workplace. Where is the corporate information saved? Is it on an intranet, in your saved files, on someone else's shared drive, or simply in the minds of your people?

Imagine an AI assistant who holds everything and uses AI to sift through and organise the data. This AI will then use natural language processing so you can simply ask for what you're looking for and enter a brief discussion to whittle it down to the precise bits of information you need.

Nothing is ever lost, duplication is removed, and a new starter could have instant access to everything. They no longer need to phone a colleague; new starters can simply 'ask AI' to get an answer on anything at any time.

The AI learns and improves over time, greatly empowering the whole workforce. As I mentioned at the end of the Story of Scout, all the technology to make her, and this a reality is already here, and these are the first examples of how it will impact our Future Of Work in the years ahead.

While we move towards the automation of the mind, we shouldn't forget our lessons from the past and the early automation that kickstarted the Industrial Revolution in the first place.

We'll continue to see Practical Robots in the form of machines replace us, with armies of droids and drones extending our factories and manufacturing environment and meaning humans become the rarer breed.

These Robots will work in construction, and other dangerous environments or will simply remove monotonous duties and tasks everywhere, from coffee shops to our service arenas.

The middle ground of using partial machines to aid human skill will continue, although it will be limited by cost. Despite being super useful, the cost of building exoskeletons to aid manual labour might outweigh the benefits they deliver.

However, these will flourish in very specialist fields, such as remote surgery or in high risk and dangerous occupations.

Let's remember our lessons from the past and rule out nothing as progress continues; costs will come down and in the case of the exoskeleton, over time who knows what practical and affordable machine-aided Cobotic solutions may appear.

The driving force for future AI and Robots is already becoming big business, and their impact on our lives ahead will be significant. While we watch the debate over their final impact, staying interested and informed is a more sensible suggestion than ignoring them. Learning to work with Robots is our only realistic option.

Where steam and electricity powered the early Industrial Revolution, and computation enables our current days, the future of AI will power the next stage of our progress.

Be it powering the decisions our virtual assistant make or powering an army of droids to take over our manual tasks; they will all likely be driven by AI.

A major factor in making these technologies a reality is the connectivity they need to come alive and progress.

Currently, many solutions are purposely throttled back to ensure we can connect and manage a multitude of applications and prioritise the voice element of our communications. We all know the pain of communicating over a video call with a colleague with poor home broadband, right? As their video and voice pauses.

Making more advanced solutions available now might actually be counter-productive if it only works for half of the users.

We are at another point where technology is currently ahead of the connectivity needed to power it. Think of the iPhone without fast mobile data; it wouldn't be a great experience.

The same applies here.

Trying to deliver an AR 3D video call when we can barely hear some people's voices over a video-call would be a disaster. As high-speed connectivity roll-outs continue and wire-free, super-fast 5G become ubiquitous, our current video calls will move from grainy images, intermittent voices, and paused videos to high-definition and more immersive experiences that truly will allow us to travel without moving.

• • •

Societal Transformation of Work

Technological innovations will continue at pace, delivering a constant stream of incredible new technologies and solutions to our lives. A key focus area of development will aim to enable the hybrid workforce.

the future of us

However, technology alone does not guarantee mass adoption or true change.

We found this during lockdown as we used solutions such as Teams and Zoom to stay in touch and keep our businesses moving, yet these were not new technologies.

I saw an early version of Teams at a meeting with Microsoft back in 2016, where we used a Beta version to run a meeting between London and their Redmond site in Washington. We shared screens and video and interacted with live documents and made the 4,772 miles between us seem like feet across a meeting room.

I said to a colleague at the time, 'I think we've just seen the future' – yet it took a few more years and lockdown for us to embrace and use these solutions.

If we look to the past, technology was usually the driving lever of change. Take the introduction of machines in the mills or Robots in the production lines. Technology replaced human power, made sense, and was adopted to increase efficiencies or replace people. People were then retrained to operate the new machines.

We have a tried and tested process with history as our proof-point opportunity, yet in the case of remote working, while we already had the solutions, we didn't really use them.

Was it due to the maturity of the solutions? Was it the complexity of the technologies? Was it our attitudes to change or the habits and comforts of traditional working patterns?

We don't like change, right?

But look at the missed opportunities over those years. Businesses could have used video call solutions to reduce their property estates and travel expenditure by half and accessed talent previously locked out of the workforce. Or we as individuals could have regained a better work life balance in our busy lives.

Surely the leadership teams and shareholders should have seen the potential and embraced these technologies, just as our ancestors did. Have modern industries lost their innovative edge? Or is this a transition point that will bring a future of societally-driven transformation as people and generations now better understand the power of technology and the opportunities it can bring to aid and improve their lives – especially in work?

This example of our experiences during lockdown has led to an unprecedented transformation in what we do and how we do it.

Let's now explore its impacts.

The Process of Work

As we look back at history, we see a continuous pattern of improving working conditions; machines replaced the dangerous and labour-intensive roles of the early stages of the Industrial Revolution, and governments took action to rebalance the lives of the workforce by introducing reduced hours and a shorter week.

A focus on well-being is what has brought us to what we consider today as reasonable work.

The majority of us took our steps into the world of work after observing the patterns and work ethic of our parents and managers, and mentors showed us the ropes in our chosen careers.

We shadowed their every move and learnt our roles and the patterns of work within the organisations, seeing the office as the home and hub of our function of work.

Technology continuously aids and assists our lives and eventually releases work from the confines of a physical office or set hours. Work truly became something we do and not somewhere we go.

Now, if we pause and reflect on our recent history, you might ask yourself: did we take things too far? Are *we* the working generations to buck the trends of continuously improving working conditions?

Had we sleep-walked into unhealthy patterns? Had we used technology not as a supportive solution as originally designed but instead to further blur the line between work and personal time? So, how do we now use technology to not only rebalance our working lives but to take us forward to the next stage?

Rebalance

As we continue to find balance in our working lives and experiment with flexible and hybrid working patterns, many will reflect and wince with a degree of regret at some of the patterns we had previously adopted, fallen into, and classed as normal. We were possibly the generations that unintentionally used progress in technology to make our lives harder, not easier.

Corporate cultures of first in the office and last to leave pushed us from the nine to five to the eight to six as fashions of 'greed is good' filled movie screens during the 1980s, coupled with an ambition to 'have it all' setting the pace for others to follow, as industry leaders and Governments alike quickly embraced the trends and established these as the minimum standards and expectations across the board.

Supported at the time by high unemployment and a competitive jobs market, society quickly fell in line and accepted these as the new normal across entire workforces and industries.

This became the zeitgeist of our time, coupled with ambition, opportunity and calls for greater equality moved us subconsciously moving form needing a single income to support a household to two.

Life for single people became difficult as the cost of living increased to accommodate double incomes, and in family circles, a whole industry of childcare was created. This subtle but significant change created an irreversible reality in which two salaries are the minimum for a fairly standard quality of life.

the future of work

During the early 2000s, technologies arrived to bring balance to this alongside claims these would free us from the office and allow us to access work anywhere.

In most cases, technology actually had an adverse impact over time. Early devices gave us remote access to systems such as email and brought incredible efficiency and improvement to our lives. We no longer needed to sit behind a desk in an office to get stuff done or stay in touch.

Freedom, right?

Well, not quite.

This access again took us further from the nine to five and formed an 'always on' culture. For many, this became an expected reality and an extension of the working day, flying against the flexible tool it was intended to be.

And while we enjoyed the freedom initially, the culture quickly captured our time and attention. Our work became the first thing we saw in the morning and the last thing we saw before sleep. We began 'glancing' at our device out of fear of missing out.

Did these innovations improve our working lives, or did they simply set new expectations?

I fondly remember having my mum and dad's time. They worked sensible hours with a single main income, and I had their attention away from technology. How did we let this slip so far out of balance as a society?

Again, you will find no bigger advocate for the good technology can and does do than me. But I'll act as our collective consciousness on this point, calling out that while we certainly embraced technology overall, we also fell into some very bad habits along the way.

'Technology should have always been about working smarter, not harder.'

And now, as many politicians and industry leaders call for a full return to the office, the vast majority are still reflecting back on their chaotic pre-pandemic life and are re-evaluating their workloads and working hours.

As a result, the main driver of the Great Resignation is likely to be one of the most significant chapters in our future history books.

The actual levers for change vary. Some simply enjoyed a different pace of life after removing the stress of the daily commute, and others enjoyed spending more time with family or investing in their health or education. For many, it's brought a practical necessity and efficiency as we've been able to get far more done through using technology to work far smarter.

> 'We will go down in history as the generation that overworked due to technology.'

So, how might technology, coupled with societal change, see the transformation of the very premise of work ahead?

• • •

The death of the nine to five

During my career, I've witnessed the introduction of modern office computing, personal computing, and the growth of mobile devices. For me, these are the key drivers of our current stage of change and transformation.

Collectively, these devices allow us to access work regardless of our physical location and conduct our business from anywhere in the world and at any time of day.

The natural progress of Moore's Law has seen devices reduce in size and double in power every couple of years until we reach the point we're at today, where you can hold a device in your pocket with 100,000 times the computation power of the computers that took Neil Armstrong to the moon.

While we focused on the power of our now well-established and useable mobility solutions, it begs the question of why we still follow the nine to five routines.

the future of work

This is a working pattern now approaching almost a hundred years old. In fact, as we explored earlier, the mobility of this technology suggests we'd already slipped from this model some time ago as we moved to become the 'always on' generation and worked harder, not smarter.

As many now balance the comfort and convenience of our home offices to get stuff done with selected days in the office, we now ask: how do we buy the efficiencies of our new working lives back now that we can afford more time for ourselves?

As some organisations introduce five- or six-hour days (or even three- or four-day weeks), is this an opportunity for radical change, or will others manage it locally and afford themselves a decent lunch break, trip to the gym, and a later start or early finishes?

There's also the question of whether business leaders will adapt their models in a bid to attract new talent, considering the Great Resignation.

Personally, I'm settling into a reasonable pattern that works for me. I use the office twice a week to collaborate and socialise and work super efficiently from my home office or see customers on the remaining three days.

I'm guilty of massively overworking, but I do try to buy a little time back for myself when I can to focus on my fitness, personal development, and family. Overall, it's working out really well for me. I wouldn't say no to a four-day week, but I don't think I'd change organisations simply to incorporate it just yet.

Flexibility is of higher importance to me, but I do predict the four-day week will make sense as AI helps us do more and will ultimately eventually become the new normal in the future for many.

However, mark my words; this transition will not be straightforward. If we are to move to more flexible patterns of working days or hours, how do we measure productivity when we are not altogether, as people choose different working hours or patterns that suit them?

And actually, the bigger question is whether we should even try to or whether we should use this opportunity to move purely to managing outputs and key performance indicators instead.

While society may have slipped into some inefficient and unhealthy practices over time, the office didn't need to slip – it was already there!

Being present in an office for eight to ten hours a day is no gauge or barometer of efficiency. It's suggested that around only 45% of our time in the office is actually productive. The other 55% is spent getting our workstations organised, grabbing a coffee to recalibrate after our commutes, catching up with colleagues, tap-on-the-shoulder interruptions, or drifting into social media posts, a message thread on our phones, or taking flight to do the famous 'on-a-phone-call walk' around the building.

You know who you are!

Now, to be super clear, I'm a big fan of the office.

I still think it has a very important role in the Future Of Work, and I make it work well for me. However, if we compare our previous working day in the office to the efficiencies of remote working without distractions, remote working can and has brought incredible efficiencies to our lives.

Many people now even suggest that they couldn't actually afford the time to travel and work in the office every day, even if they wanted to.

However, old habits will die hard for many, and numerous leaders and organisations will struggle to move from presenteeism and traditional-hours-worked models to one measured in outputs. But, thankfully, AI is already beginning to support work management and will likely run our projects completely and provide a complete stat and audit trail in future, reporting who has done what and for how long on a project or task.

• • •

Changing Attitudes to Work

While technology and a pandemic have brought an unprecedented point of reflection and consideration for many, and these are clearly significant drivers of change, the real change in the Future Of Us will fall to us.

As explored in Chapter 4, for the first time in history, we currently have four generations in the workforce, with a fifth closely on their way.

Each of these will bring a slightly different viewpoint, experience, and opinion on how work should be done, and with far stronger expectations on what will and won't work for them. Ultimately, this combination of experiences and new attitudes will start the most important transformation of work we've seen so far.

Regardless of which generation our age places us in, there are currently three key overriding attitudes to work in play that are quietly but rapidly changing the shape and face of work as we know it. We fall into three main groups

Firstly, the **Stick to What We Know** gang. This group have built some truly incredible organisations and enjoyed sometimes bumpy but overall good careers. Taking the baton from the elders of industry, following tried-and-tested processes, and mirroring working patterns, this group aims toward progress alongside the comforts of stability. Each wave brings gradual improvements through driven ambitions and sheer hard work.

Secondly, the **Equilibrium Army**. In stark contrast to the views and ambitions of the above group, this group holds the jobs and needs the jobs but doesn't necessarily want the jobs.

They see work as a means to an end and proactively balance between work and often seek far greater fulfilment outside of their working lives or corporate worlds.

Often highly educated individuals with far wider political and economic understandings. We could argue these are the healthiest group in terms of attitudes and well-being; they will resist and challenge the principles of many capitalist and corporate organisations, inputting what is required and using the system to work for them from a survival and stability perspective.

They will resist the team-building cultures of the corporate L&D drives and instead join online communities and social media groups. The subtle but rising Anti-work movements and attitudes will collectively grow and empower their cause and, over time, will likely hold the majority in some way.

Overall, only organisations with incredibly strong brands, purpose, and cultures will be able to retain or attract them.

Finally, the **New Way Workers**. Educated and likely self-taught in a field of their interest or hobby, this group are usually informed, knowledgeable, and tech-savvy workers who are self-motivated and keen to progress.

Though they want to do it their way, even if they don't actually have an initial plan of direction. While we may naturally expect them to sit in the younger generations, the early adopters we referenced in Chapter 3 will likely fall into this category and adopt any interesting new ways of working.

This group will likely have niche or in-demand skills, know their worth, and will value the time and location of their work over pure outright financial reward. Competition for their skills will see a natural premium scale aid them to have the best of both worlds.

They will hold a very strong voice in the battle for talent, and they will clearly set out what is and isn't going to work for them. They will vote quickly with their feet as their loyalty will quite rightly be to themselves.

This last group may hold the strongest driver for real change of the three, and elements of their attitudes and approach will be of appeal and recognised by others who aspire to join or support their cause to fuel collective action and real change.

You may feel there is a natural bias or promotion to the New Way Worker in my wording, and while I acknowledge some of these traits resonate with my own approach, I will stress that no one group is right or wrong here.

The values and attitudes of all three groups are essential to bringing balance to the Future Of Work. We could argue the Equilibrium Army's views may be a better fit in our current circumstances, as why should we give more than is asked of us?

We don't overpay in shops, right? So, why do we give our value of time for free?

But, whichever lens we look at it through, they are collectively equally important. Each group acts as a stabiliser and leveller and collectively ensures we all keep on track and ensures we don't slip back into unhealthy work habits.

• • •

Where We Work

So, are we remote, flexible, agile, dynamic, or hybrid?

Well, while we settle on a name for the future of the workforce learning to make the best use of Digital Solutions, let's now look at where we are likely to carry out our work in the future.

As only around 35% of the workforce is expected to return to the office full-time, and as the world of business builds a Future Of Work that is virtual, accessible anywhere, and gives us mobile devices to access the company's services we need to do our jobs, the question is: why do we even need an office?

And where else might we reside to carry out our roles?

Let's look at some of the options available.

Our First Space

Habit sees the majority of us instantly associate work with a physical location, such as an office, city, store, or industrial environment. Yet as we exit Covid and our offices still remain largely empty, we now have a view that our homes are our prime locations of work.

We've commandeered spare rooms equipped with new desks, additional monitors, comfy chairs, and an array of accessories – from HD webcams to advanced noise-cancelling speakers and headphones. Or we take over dining tables or bedrooms with pack-away workplaces that we prepare every morning and hide in the evening.

Our homes and our offices will evolve to cater for this new way of living and working. New homes will be built with multifunctional rooms, using partitions and hideaway panels to reveal monitors or projectors to cast a screen instantly and allow private calls without taking over a room for dedicated use.

And while many have managed to work from home during lockdown, using spare rooms, dining tables, desks in bedrooms, or invested in a garden office, not everyone can realistically work from home, nor do they necessarily want to.

Social isolation alone means that heading into the office every now and again is essential for our well-being and sanity. We are social creatures by design, and interactions are an essential aspect of our health.

Also, a year into lockdown, I worked on a number of collaboration projects using impressive online tools with virtual whiteboards and post-it notes in an attempt to replicate a physical workshop.

We will also likely see more pre-meeting lobbies where you can set a little time ahead of the meeting to allow people to use the bathroom or refresh a coffee, or simply chat as though they would at the start of a physical meeting. The water cooler places we currently miss in our back-to-back virtual calendar meeting worlds.

Overall, I have to say I'm pretty impressed with the tech, but given a choice, for more in-depth workshop style collaborations, I'd take the physical version in a heartbeat. The time before and after these workshops allows us the opportunity to chat and socialise over a coffee break, and lunches are sorely missed as we lack the subsequent knowledge exchanges that occur in these physical environments.

Our Second Space – *the office of the future*

As we consciously or subconsciously demote the office into second place, what will become of these now emptier spaces, and how will the office of the future look?

Be it a lack of space, privacy, connectivity, or simply personal preferences on how we work, the role of the office still plays a very important role for the majority of us.

While the majority don't use it as often as they did previously, people are now clearer on the role it plays and how they can make it best work for them.

Be it for those that continue to use it as their primary workplace due to lack of space in their homes, reliability of connectivity, other technologies, or simply a personal preference. Through to those that instead either look to vary their week, choosing to mix up their routine with a few days at home balanced with a few days in the office and the company of others. Or the rarer visitors who want to come to the office to collaborate on a specific task or project, leaving their laptops at home and bringing a more social and a novelty feel to these rarer visits.

Desks in offices will be replaced with single user booths, and larger collaboration spaces will replace the line of small, cramped meeting rooms. These bigger spaces will use advanced projection or multiple screens on walls to seamlessly integrate both physical and virtual attendees.

To address these varying user groups preferences, organisations have redesigned (or are still planning to redesign) their spaces to cater for these different user groups and balance enough fixed desks with wider collaboration spaces and more social environments.

The general consensus is that overall property estates will reduce by around half, and more shared spaces will appear to address the uncertain demand as we all navigate the future of working models.

We will also see the growth of dedicated meeting technologies with multi-screen and digital interactive whiteboards allowing us to beam guests into physical space in a more involving and interactive feel. HD Video, 3D AR, Spatial Audio and projection technologies will make the experience far more involving and encourage people to use these types of solutions for certain tasks and projects. They will be expensive, limited in numbers but an incredible experience for users.

We will also see an increase in on-site filming studios and media rooms at our main sites. If you and your customer are more virtual, how do you best present your business and teams in a high-quality and professional way on important engagements and interactions?

By bringing them into a studio to film or present live broadcasts. Presentations and sales pitches to audiences anywhere will bring a more professional feel and avoid the risk of technical difficulties or real-life disruptions.

As we split the workforce between physical and virtual locations, these meeting solutions will evolve and use features such as auto presence technology, making decisions on whether you join using your video, picture, or avatar due to bandwidths available at the time, switching up and down instantly, constantly improving our experience.

the future of work

Third spaces – *the drop zones*

As we adjust to hybrid work patterns and our companies review and reduce their properties' estates, we will make great use of ad hoc work locations, such as coffee shops or the Office As A Service model.

There is no shortage of coffee shops, and we've seen some great innovations as many have evolved their models brilliantly to cater for our new ways of working over the years.

They've redesigned their spaces to provide for our need for privacy with chairs backed up to walls to give us plain video call backdrops and multiple single seats to make good use of spaces, great Wi-Fi, an array of charging options, and, of course, great coffee. Some even see staff offering to watch your temporary working set-up while you nip to the toilet ... A side effect of all that great tea and coffee.

While this is great and serves a fantastic purpose, the future of this Third Space will also evolve to see more closed booths or pods for private and reduced background noise video calls and the Office As A Service model will evolve to allow you to hire a desk, booth or pod by the hour or day, as well as the default monthly option.

This isn't a new model, but it does need a little tweaking to truly cater for the Future Of Work; otherwise, it's just someone else's office. While your organisation might remove the hassle of managing spaces, the costs will likely be equalled, which is a missed opportunity to reduce them in the first place.

The other side to this opportunity is the reality that we don't always know someone's location when we set up calls: are they travelling or between meetings?

Joining a video call while on the move isn't a great experience for anyone as we are now finding.

What we need is an array of these booths, pods scattered across our cities, in coffee shops, train stations, or in the growing number of empty premise, providing somewhere we can go while on the move. A modern phone booth, in theory.

This would be a great solution for the millions of people adapting to and trying to manage hybrid working. Offer a comfy chair, clean toilet, super-fast connectivity, a charger, and refreshment on a pay-as-you-go, by-the-hour model.

I'm sure it's already in the plans for many Office As A Service provider or property owners in key locations and travel hubs, but I would say hurry up if you're reading this. We need this gap filled quickly.

Fourth Space – *travel without moving*

Technology is always a vehicle for change, and our time will be no different. Developments and progress in fields such as Virtual and Augmented Reality will see new ways to collaborate and meet.

Huge investments are currently being made to develop these solutions as the main tech providers and start-ups alike look for killer applications for both social and work applications.

And again, while not a new technology, the overall uptake of VR, in general, is still very low. However, as with all technology, it's likely to continuously improve – who knows what exciting solutions may come to market over the years ahead and with considerable recent progress in AR solutions we could see that 'Window to Work' via XR become a reality far quickly that many realise

But are we missing a trick in the short term? I join a number of VR meetings every week, and while I would struggle to stay in a VR headset for long periods of time, it's a great experience to join a couple of short sessions, and it's a useful tool for very focused engagements.

Hands up, who multitasks while listening to video calls or streamed updates from your exec?

Yep, you know who you are.

You nip into your emails, take a quick look at your phones, or jump on the Internet, but you were still listening, right? Or we use the 'Sorry, could you say that again it broke up my side' line to cover the fact that we simply weren't listening.

XR solutions are far more immersive; therefore, great for capturing someone's full attention. Know that you cannot multitask... I'll come back to this later.

The Fifth Space – the field force

As the news headlines provide coverage of the future of the office, what of our field workers? We have armies of experts and specialists keeping the wheels of industry and services running across the world; the large majority of these people may never set foot in an office yet have been quietly using remote solutions for many years to access job sheets and information.

Advances in Robotics and a crossover between physical and virtual worlds will evolve the field work as we know it.

We will build digital twins of locations and services, litter millions of assets with sensors and IoT solutions, and then access them virtually via VR or AR solutions.

In theory, this will allow you to work remotely using on-site or drafted-in Robotics to do the work while you're miles away sitting in your house with a cup of tea. As Robotics technologies progress, coupled with ubiquitous high-speed connectivity connecting remote workers with remote Robots, this will likely provide the ingredients of a very significant point of history in the transformation of us as we see the whispered Rise of the Machines.

• • •

Access to Work

These changes to how we work will provide greater options to those previously locked out of the 'traditional' working practices.

While we previously may have had the choice and ability to do daily commutes and nine to five shifts, this wasn't the case for everyone. Millions of people across the world are locked out of the workforce due to childcare commitments, neurodiversity, being disabled, mental health issues, or caring commitments.

As technology now allows us to work from anywhere, and new attitudes and approaches to work allow us more flexible hours, is this an overlooked opportunity to open access to work to people previously locked out of the workforce?

Furthermore, does this also allow people to take new approaches to their careers and take time out to raise a family or to retrain coupling a mix of work and study?

The need to fit around children's school schedules has locked millions of parents out of work for many years when most only needed to be able to do the school run in the morning and mid-afternoon. This should have never been a barrier to work in our supposedly modern world.

Also, while many of you reading this may be able to successfully attend an interview with little more than some late-night preparation and the usual interview nerves, join a firm as the new guy with your wits about you, and navigate office politics while getting to know your new colleagues, this is incredibly difficult for many for a range of reasons – from juggling caring commitments, neurodiversity or being disabled

Are our new ways of working now opening the field and allowing us to interview in more comfortable virtual environments and work in practice in more varied and suitable ways?

Are we missing out on some incredible talent that was previously locked out? I think we are!

What about the millions of dyslexic thinkers who may not have been able to make the traditional paper shifts or bring the plethora of qualifications needed but whose creativity and logical thinking skills, interpersonal, communication, and story-telling skills are truly incredible?

Or the autistic genius whose deep focus, observational skills, attention to detail, and thoroughness would likely trump the minds of your very best employees today yet who may struggle with the social and interaction skills to make those 'traditional' working models a viable option.

Hmm, a sensitive topic? *Too* sensitive? Rubbish! This is about fair inclusion, and we need to lose the fear in addressing this topic and start making it happen now.

Digital Inclusion is everyone's responsibility. This goes way beyond inclusion; we are all different, not lesser, and here technology is giving us the opportunity to level the playing field. It is giving us all an opportunity to embrace it positively. We can not miss this opportunity!

The Future of Learning

We leave education prepared for work. Well, that's the theory. The reality is that while it equips us with the basics and our common language of communication and understanding across our industries, the majority of what we do in our day jobs, we learn on the job.

And if we consider everything we've covered so far, the common thread here is that we absolutely need to focus on our learning to understand what new solutions and technologies are going to either impact our industries or jobs on a day-to-day basis.

But who owns our development? Do you have time in your diary to read, learn, and research? Or do you sigh when you see the email from L&D inviting you to a course or training session, or the reminder of the soon-to-expire mandatory compliance course, concerned they're going to eat time you just don't have?

As technology evolves and the pace increases, we will have no choice but to constantly up-skill to stay relevant or just to work alongside new technologies.

'The future of work consists of learning a living.'
Marshall McLuhan

Yet how many days this year have you spent on your own learning? I will cover this in much more detail later, but will say that learning a living is the likely reality of jobs of the future.

Gig Economy

As the Future Of Work evolves, the power and benefits of our new digital workplace tools, coupled with our changing attitudes to work, will naturally fuel growth in Gig Work. This will not purely be an alternative to full-time employment work per se, but also as a means to earn extra income as our Life As A Service costs increase or to de-risk our reliance on a single income or organisation.

The principles of Gig Work are far from new, as people have freelanced their skills and expertise for many years across industries. These people prefer flexibility while balancing the uncertainties of possible gaps in employment and short-term contracts.

Now, as the Great Resignation continues and the jobs market remains buoyant, talent is scarce for organisations. Gig Work may bring a mutually appealing opportunity to both employees and employers in the Future Of Work.

The key drivers will be:

→ **Choice:** The skills, knowledge, and value awareness will allow those with the skills the opportunity to make choices.

They will first make a choice based on their own personal preferences: are they ambitious and looking to build a business in this space? Or are they looking for a lifestyle job that allows them the choice of when they work and where? The value of this from a work-life balance and reduced cost of childcare perspective is not to be overlooked.

→ **Skills Gap:** Those with the skills required for the new digital roles, or roles in demand, will become valuable assets. They will quickly realise their worth, and it will become difficult for companies to retain their talent.

Also, the growing skill demand will catch many companies napping, and by the time they realise the in-demand skills, either the employee will have left, or a more progressive organisation will have lured them over.

→ **Rare Skill:** Aside from the obvious value of holding a rare skill when working for an organisation, rare skills in the Gig Economy will often be sought by many and will see people working across a number of contracts at the same time.

Digital Technology and applications will also aim to make these Gigs easier to find and allows the efficient partitioning of project tasks and contracts. Wide ranges of project management tools incorporating AI are now available, allowing far greater collaboration between an organisations employees and Gig workers.

→ **Replicable Work:** We will also see people able to sell work they've already done to other organisations with a similar need. As we speak, many people will be working on a project or task for organisations that could be used by others.

Gig Work will allow people to look at job ads/requests and quickly adapt existing works to fit new customers' needs. In theory, this may see us working for two or three organisations at the same time, using replicable or pre completed work.

→ **Technology:** As a now pretty mature field, there is a wide range of Gig applications such as TaskRabbit, Mechanical Turk, and Fiverr that bring expert skills and organisations together via easy-to-use applications.

I used Gig applications to design the cover of this book, create artwork for my website, photography at my live events, and a wonderful editor edited this book, all via Gig applications.

Technology will further advance as AI continue to support projects and tasks.

There are natural integrations into Gig Work where a skill or role is missing in a project for whatever reason. AI solutions will allow the gap to be advertised or linked into one of the existing Gig applications to find a skills match, and AI will then partition work in safe and secure areas, so the Gig Worker only sees what's needed and relevant. This will mutually benefit both parties and is likely to transform the jobs market further.

→ **Brand & Reputation:** Aside from the lifestyle choices we take in making the Gig Economy work for us, we will also see a rise in people (particularly those with skills in demand) actively looking to work for organisations whose brand purpose and cause are a match with the individual's principles, morals, or beliefs.

What does the organisation stand for, and why should we work for them? Are they a charity or a political organisation we wish to support? Or are they a super cool upcoming tech company that we want to be associated with?

A company's brand and reputation will grow evermore important when it comes to not only attracting and retaining full-time talent but also the Gig Workforce.

→ **Alternative Income:** As the cost-of-living increases, many will turn to Gig Work as an opportunity to gain extra income, utilising both skills and available time to great effect. Gig will provide a great opportunity to earn extra income in a super convenient way.

→ **Stability:** While the very premise of Gig Work suggests anything but stability, it will, in fact, bring a degree of control over both people's destiny and their income.

The need to acquire various income streams will grow in importance as many use Gig Work to vary their income streams and de-risk any fluctuations in their main employment. No more jobs for life. The Gig Economy offers people a fallback that provides additional income and is there for them if they lose their primary income.

→ **Retirement:** When do you plan to retire? Do you have a plan? What income, savings, and investments do you need to retire? How will increased costs of living and the rising cost of our digital lives impact your plans? I will pay close focus to this in the next chapter. The rising cost of living and increased costs of Digital Services will transform retirement as we know it and massively fuel the Gig Economy.

> *'The Future Of Work will have no retirement age, we'll just have more choice of what we do and when we do it.'*

Retirement working is a great fit for Gig Workers as this group are unlikely to be looking for the security of long-term fixed contracts and instead seek the flexibility of short-term income top-ups that fit a more relaxed work schedule.

Most retired people would love this option, the flexibility, and the ability to 'stay in the game' a little longer.

Technology and Gig Work could provide not only a perfect option but also massively support the current Great Resignation as employers reduce their risk and costs in utilising this new access to talent.

→ **Inclusion & Equality:** Building on employing the retired workforce and the points explored in the Access to Work section earlier, digital tools will massively support the whole Digital Inclusion and equality focus.

I hired my Gig Workforce to support my side hustle and the publication of this book based on their recommendations and ratings. I have no idea what these people look like, their age, their gender, their personal situations of why they work in Gig, or their locations. They could be 18 or 80, working full-time and doing my stuff in their spare time; who cares about that if we're happy with their ratings and the work they do?

The Gig Economy will unconsciously positively support the whole Digital Inclusion agenda, and long may it continue.

→ **Reporting & Managing:** Advances in digital communication and collaboration software incorporating AI and Machine Learning will be what really accelerate Gig Workers from the current small percentage of highly skilled individuals, staying ahead of the skills gap, or businesses looking to stay agile in managing workload demand, into the new normal.

These technology solutions will see AI take the lead and allow a department to run a project and see exactly who is involved, who worked on what, and which tasks require collaboration.

A dashboard and the AI will be able to report on projects' progress, call out any delays, and highlight the need for skills – as well as who has them within the project. Where there is a gap, it can look to acquire these in a single sub-project, farming tasks out securely in isolation to the Gig Economy.

These new types of AI project systems will report exactly who did what and when and acknowledge performance or pay as required. Projects will become far more efficient, and the days of lazy co-workers you carry through a project will be a thing of the past.

• • •

The Future of Management

'So much of what we call management consists of making it difficult for people to work.'
Peter Drucker

So, as how we work, where we work, and our attitudes to work all transform, how on earth do we manage, and be managed, in work?

The majority of people, as the saying goes, 'simply want to do a fair day's work for a fair day's pay' and approach their work with a high degree of integrity, personal pride, and ambition to progress in their careers.

So, what do we expect from management and leadership teams of the future? And, in turn, what might they expect from us?

There is no shortage of management guidebooks or courses organisations can send their people on to help them develop their management skills and performance.

But the majority of managers in our organisations often have no formal training or qualifications in people management. Yet, while we might lead our businesses as mainly amateur managers, and I can hear the management community saying 'ouch' at this statement, let me add that overall, we do a pretty good job.

I've personally had the pleasure of working with some incredible leaders over my career who've learnt from examples and experiences backed up with common sense and personal skills you could never teach. They've honed their skills and approaches over time and possess the key skill of adaptability. They adjust their styles based on the different personalities within teams and become masters of flexibility.

And yes, we all have a horror story of working for a shocking manager or those who've left a decent organisation or team purely to escape a poor manager who simple lacked the skill and experience needed to support us.

But how do we now adjust the skills we've learnt over many years to manage and *be* managed in a remote and virtual world?

Firstly, this is a two-way street. Working flat-out or being a busy fool isn't a measure of your productivity. We should work with our leadership teams to understand the focus areas and how we collectively work towards our goals, and what our tasks and measures will be. Management is about success agreements and direction, not time management.

Most of us don't need managing, just leading and supporting. I hate the word. I think of my current leader (who is simply brilliant) as my guide, my sounding board, and my critical friend who empowers me to do a better job. All values which enable and empower me in my role.

The very thought of him asking what I'm doing in terms of my time or productivity would horrify us both, I'm sure. My point here is as our working environments are changing, the KPIs aren't. We still have the same jobs to do and the same businesses to run, so now, how do we beneficially adjust our management methods in our more remote worlds?

As our locations change and we use our new environments to adjust what times we work, the old measures of hours worked are completely losing their suitability as a measure of productivity. And again, not to dress this up, but if – as we explored earlier – only around 45% of people's time in the office is actually productive, we could argue that measuring hours worked wasn't really fit for purpose in many occupations anyway.

I once watched a guy in the office surf the Internet for a whole day, his screen never once showing anything even remotely related to his work. The fact he was in the office that day was nothing more than an expense on our heating bill. Would an agreement of work/expectations addressed this?

Sure, I get that we need to have some framework of understanding around when we work. It brings structure to our lives and gives us awareness and acceptance of when we can contact each other.

However, a large part of many of our roles is about getting stuck in and focused on a project and the outputs of our work, not how long and when we've sat in front of a screen.

It will be far more viable to move to an output-based system where we have a shared input as to the viability of a task, the expected outputs, and agreed timescales of work.

This fussy headline continually hitting newsreels around leaders wanting everyone back in the office or concerns of people kicking back at home. As covered earlier, I'm sure the office will naturally find its purpose and still play a role, but if we can't adapt to manage work remotely and need to see people to physically know if they are working or to get the best out of people, I suggest we consider new careers.

Also, technology will massively help address this and is already starting to support project management roles. AI is being used to build a team of skills, allocate work and tasks to individuals, and then report back on the inputs and efforts of each, and as mentioned early .

This transformation can't come quickly enough for the hard workers amongst us.

Have you ever felt like you're carrying a teammate? Yep, me too... Well, moving to these AI and output measures systems will bring a far greater, fairer, and more efficient system for all.

> *'Stop managing productivity,*
> *start to measure outputs.'*

The reality is we're not going back to the old ways; it makes no sense in a time of incredible technology as changing views on our values and purpose. History proves the success of the Future Of Us will be built by the organisations and people that can accept new trends and adapt to form cultures that people get and want to be part of.

Employment levels will rise and fall over time for a number of reasons, and we will always see plentiful job markets followed by rising unemployment. It's a two-way street, and organisations of the future will not be able to carry the lazy, nor will advances in AI allow them to.

• • •

Organisations of the Future

As we adjust to our new ways of working, we will naturally look to work for and with organisations with strong brands, clear purpose, brilliant cultures, and size and scale, suggesting the stability of long-term employment where possible.

We want the flexibility of these new ways of working, but we also naturally crave the stability of longer-term tenures in big, well-known organisations. So, it's important to make the right choice when deciding who to work for.

Rarely do we consider whether these big organisations will stand the test of time and survive their own digital evolutions. The future is not only about our own relevance; the reality is that many of our beloved brands and organisations of today will not stand the test of time and survive the Digital Transformation.

> *'Digital is the main reason just over half the companies on the Fortune 500 have disappeared since 2000.'*
> **Pierre Nanterme** – CEO Accenture

So, what limits an organisation's ability to transform, evolve, and stay relevant?

Feels a little dramatic, sure, but as the pace picks up, not all organisations will be able to evolve or respond in time. This doesn't necessarily mean they will go bust, but when the going gets tough, savings and cutbacks often follow.

Firstly, an aversion to risk and the mass of governance processes to manage and mitigate risk results in most organisations being far from agile.

I've worked in the corporate world for most of my life, so I've seen both sensible and excessive risk-management processes. Some made sense, and others felt like we were creating work and jobs for the sake of it. They were more focused on the process than the actual risk it was designed to manage.

As a result of complicated risk management procedures, it can take an average of around 320 days for a corporate organisation to launch new solutions or products. Close to a year in the current world feels like a long time, and in our fast-paced future, it will feel like an eternity.

Secondly, while they might not be looking forward, organisations need to explore new areas of innovation.

Many company boards are answerable to shareholders or Investors, and unless it's a charitable cause, profit is king. This usually cascades downwards very smoothly through the organisation by way of target packs, and KPIs and success are heavily weighted, if not totally measured, against them.

This focus on commercial trading is critically important for sure; we need to sustain our commercial organisations. But while we crack on with our heads down to deliver 'the numbers', do organisations also have the means to see and assess the wider factors of change and transformation in play?

Often not.

And it's not just about missing risks – it's also about missing opportunities.

Blockbuster were at the top of their game when they passed up the chance to buy Netflix's in 2000, who had just turned down an offer from Amazon. There are a number of versions of events from those early meetings, from suggestions that Blockbuster executives had to resist laughing at their valuation of £50m, and alleged comments that they didn't see them as a real competitor or threat.

When Blockbuster closed the door on their final store in 2019, Netflix's hit a value of $20bn and peaked at $29bn in 2021.

This point brings me to the final and most important point here.

Do organisations have a process to really understand and manage innovation and wider disintermediation?

How do organisations assess and evaluate disruption way beyond the usual competitor analysis?

Existing market analysis certainly didn't help Blockbuster or many retailers in the case of Amazon's growth, the motor industry in the case of Tesla, or the hotel industry in the case of Airbnb.

Innovation analysis needs to consider far wider drivers of change in the future, such as disruptive start-ups, societal evolution, and the collisions of technology we mentioned earlier. Netflix's idea wasn't anything without super-fast broadband in everyone's home. Of course, this wasn't a reality at the time of the Blockbuster conversation, yet the technologies had already arrived.

Instead, this was about exploring the 'what if's' and applying a future lens, not looking at the direct competitors.

Business innovation, opportunity creation, and de-risking disintermediation is a whole book in itself, and I will pause here and close this chapter by saying that moving companies and roles is tough for anyone. While we might swap and change roles far more in the future, let's make that our own choices and not presume that the business we're working for is heading in the wrong direction or doesn't make the grade.

Remember, an interview is a two-way process. Ask questions about their strategy and do your research.

What are their plans and focus?

Do they feel like a trading engine, only interested in short-term results, or do you see visions and plans for evolution and innovation cultures in line with your visions or everything we have covered so far?

Take Aways & Points to Consider

- We have four generations in the workforce today, all with different views, opinions, and attitudes towards work. Together, we will shape the Future Of Work.

- A plethora of new technologies will appear that aid and improve our working lives, but they won't be without issues and challenges as more services and processes become automated.

- We might ask whether the Robots will take our jobs. While the debate continues to divide experts, whatever the outcome, we should expect a significant impact on our role and the introduction of CoBotics as a likely outcome.

- We will likely have multiple employers in the Future Of Work, with more Gig-Economy type models embraces or offered by organisations to support improved work-life balance, shape new careers, diversify incomes, or top-up salaries.

- Not every business will make the next stage of the Digital Revolution. We need to carefully select the organisations we choose to work for to limit the expected disruption ahead.

- As our world of work evolved, so too must our skills. Learning new skills will become critical as we begin to learn our livings.

- Ask your employer for their thoughts and plans on the Future Of Work for your organisation. They may not have reached a final model, but find out what their current thinking is.

- Ask to join any pilot or test scheme they have or may be planning. It's a two-way street – input from both sides is essential, and you could play a positive role in helping to shape the Future Of Work for your organisation, regardless how big or small.

'It's only a few pounds a month, right?'

7
life as a service

*'The Revolution will not be televised…
it will be streamed and charged monthly to a device of your choice.'*

life as a service

As work evolves and we consider our roles and how we might earn our living in the future, we also need to consider what we might need to fund the *costs* of our lives.

This increased cost of living comes not only from rising inflation and energy costs but the addition of more Digital Services 'at a cost' in our lives.

Take a look at your bank statement. We all appear to be collecting an increasing number of recurring monthly and ad hoc digital transactions.

While we might nod in recognition to a lot of these, many need a little more thought, or even research, before we remember what they are and what they do for us.

I'll share here my monthly digital costs and thoughts on each one.

(I may not mention all the provider names, and I have factored annual fees to show a monthly cost for the purpose of this example.)

- **£67 p/m:** Super-fast broadband connecting all our devices and allowing us to work, game, and consume a heap of media in every room. This is the access point to our digital worlds.

- **£132 p/m:** Mobile phones for the family. We could lose our TVs and computers, but not our digital remote controls.

- **£13.25 p/m:** TV licence. I don't remember the last time I actually watched TV, but I guess we're stuck with this one for now.

- **£10.99 p/m:** A popular media streaming site that provides me with HD films at home and during train journeys.

- **£8.99 p/m:** Another TV streaming site, but this one gives me music and free delivery on parcels. This is an incredible service in our lives; it's far from cheap, but proof that we are willing to pay for convenience.

the future of us

- **£7.99 p/m:** With this, I can listen to a vast range of audiobooks. Listening to these while I walk the dog this is great solution.

- **£16.99 p/m:** Unlimited ad-free music for all our family devices; as big music fans, we really make the most of this service, tracking a daily usage of around three hours.

- **£6.67 p/m:** Photo and home movie storage. It automatically backs up every picture we take onto the cloud. Ultimately, this is now our memory bank, and we could never switch this service off. Ultimately, we no longer own our memories. Scary thought, right?

- **£3 p/m:** This provides extra storage space on my family's devices and cloud back-ups.

- **£65 p/m:** This provides a mass of gaming services for the kids. Providing access to games catalogues, online collaboration game play and chat facilities. The price of this explains why the gaming industry is worth more than the music and film industries combined.

- **£6.58 p/m:** Our family office applications on our laptops and devices come in at £79 per year (Word, Excel, etc.). There are free alternatives, but these are familiar and consistent with our work and school solutions and, again, convenient.

- **£19.99 p/m:** Our home live-monitoring alarm system. This is connected to a mass of sensors in our smart home, giving us peace of mind while out of the house.

- **£8.75 p/m:** This ensures my car has the latest Sat Nav updates, with live traffic and route guidance. Not sure I need this anymore with the reduction in car travel since lockdown and the free services on smart devices.

life as a service

- **£39.99 p/m:** As a family of budding photographers, including one professional, we pay for premium photo-editing software.

- **£5 p/m:** This provides a security application for a laptop I'm not even sure we still have.

- **£4.99 p/m:** Video editing software that allows us all to create video content for social media or to edit our own home movies.

- **£12.99 p/m:** An online fitness and yoga service that allows us to work out in the front room as part of our fitness regimes or for those days when we don't feel like hitting the gym. This service is a lockdown life-saver we've stuck with.

- **£33.00 p/m:** A lockdown wine club that has become a staple part of the weekly shopping.

- **£2.50 p/m:** A hiking application that we used twice and was long forgotten that I need to cancel.

- **£8.00 p/m:** A web domain and website builder that we set up for a school project and forgot to cancel.

- **£12.08 p/m:** This is the average monthly cost of the four online training courses I've bought this year. Short online courses are my preferred way to learn new technologies or focus areas of my development.

- **£10 p/m:** An online music notation application for one of the kids' schoolwork. It feels optional but really helps him, and I can see the value if it's helping him study.

- **£7.00 p/m:** To enjoy a great shave every time, new blades are delivered to my door.

The total monthly cost of my digital life is £502.75. Annually, this works out to £6,033.

So, how did yours compare?
Any surprises?
Did you recognise them all?
Now let's bring this into balance. If the average UK salary is £31,400, this equates to nearly 20% of the yearly income. Granted, we could argue that many of these are far from essential, but even after careful consideration, many services are difficult to switch off.

Surely there has to be a solution to monitor and manage these? Well, yes, there is. Innovators always find a solution to every problem. You can download applications that closely track your digital Life As A Service costs. Ironically, they do charge you a fee to do this!...of course they do, that's the pattern here right?

We could argue that some of these digital services costs replace traditional purchases we would typically make on the high street or in our regular grocery shop anyway.

Still, the point here is that even if we don't make a purchase, the service fee automatically recurs. Making it very difficult to knowingly 'cut back' as required for a month or two.

This digitisation and monetisation model extends out to almost every service we can consume or goods we can buy.

And if we are only at the start of this accelerating trend, where will it stop, and for how many months could we maintain our digital lives if we were out of work or our incomes paused?

This convenience and the instant ability to have it all has great appeal. This appeal is especially applicable as the increased cost of living is making it increasingly difficult for younger generations to save and take steps onto the housing ladder, so it is becoming the default or only option for many. The market naturally reacts, and we can now not only rent our homes – but for an additional monthly fee – pretty much every item within them.

We can rent everything from the sofas we sit on to the cutlery we eat with and the art on the walls. We can fill our wardrobes with rented clothes and have a constant supply of food and drink in the fridge and flowers on the table – all for the right monthly fee, of course. In fact, if you can name it, someone will likely be providing it as part of what I'm going to call **Life As A Service.**

I predict this trend, and the evolving patterns and attitudes towards ownership overall, is signalling the start of a period of significant societal evaluation and transformation. This transformation will have a major impact on our lives and future generations, spelling a global shift in economic models.

So, why is this happening? Simply put, we are the prize in the battle for our digital spending.

'It's only a few pounds a month, right…?'

The Battle for Our Digital Spend

First, let me be clear. This is no unconscious or coincidental theme. Some of the most significant innovations in history are not actually the products themselves but rather how brands and organisations changed the way we buy and consume their products and services.

This, or where they have intentionally created or grown a market specifically for their product.

Let's look at the motor industry as an example of both innovations.

In the 1930s, Henry Ford mass-produced a car that only a few could afford. As covered earlier his innovations resulted from his backing calls to increase wages in factories, which not only made it possible for more of his employees to buy a car but also made it an appealing place to work. Therefore, people left their jobs to go and work for Ford, fuelling increasing salaries across wider industries as others had to increase wages or lose talent.

This opened up more people who could afford his product. Ford then quickly backed the move to the five-day workweek, meaning people not only had the funds needed to buy his cars but also the leisure time to enjoy them.

These innovations didn't stop with Ford; over time, the introduction of finance options further extended the market to the masses who were previously unable to afford the luxury of a motor car.

These financial innovations progressed over time even further as factoring residual values out of high-end and luxury cars allowed people to drive cars previously out of their price range.

But I stress 'drive', not 'own', here. These innovations meant people no longer really owned cars. Instead, they leased them As A Service, which is pretty much how most people own (sorry, *drive*) a car today.

Short-term leases followed, and we can now consume and fund motoring in any way imaginable, from accessing a city car by the hour, a four-by-four for a camping trip, or a supercar as a treat for a weekend getaway.

These innovations removed the barrier of affordability, allowing us to 'have it all' whether we can 'afford it all' or not.

All these steps were purely designed and introduced to sell more cars and open up new markets of buyers that previously couldn't afford the full upfront cost of the car. However, over time, these innovations adapted to maintain and ensure recurring spending at the point of renewal.

This latter point is the ultimate aim, moving us from a one-off purchasing customer to a long-term or lifetime customer. Think about your own car, its current market value, and how you finance it.

Do you actually own any of it?

Think of your photos and memories as another example of recurring spend. We're unlikely to ever stop paying for our memories, right? With the introduction of cloud photo storage, we've become lifetime customers by default.

What are our alternatives? Do we purchase a few external hard drives and faff about backing them up every once in a while, hoping they don't break or go missing?

So, the innovation here addressed a problem by giving us peace of mind that our memories are safe. In return, companies secured our monthly spending forever 'As A Service'. Be clear that this is an intentional move and only the start of a far broader battle for our digital spend.

Funding the Future

The start-up and entrepreneur communities are further fuelling these 'As A Service' models.
Great ideas are plentiful, and, in theory, so is money.
However, the problem most start-ups have is the money to fund the idea to take it from a seed into a working and marketable solution or service.

The bits in-between the great ideas and reality of a product or service we use every day are the Investors and venture capitalist communities. These are the people who decide who gets the funding to turn their dreams into realities.
The start-up community is a busy sector with innovations far outnumbering funders.
Investors have no shortage of choices and will always carry out very careful due diligence; the chance of an idea becoming a profitable reality is often very slim.

'90% of funded start-ups fail.'

Investors will look at the market research and challenge whether there is a problem to solve, a need in the market, whether the start-up's unique, whether this is a space they know, whether people will buy it and how, and, most importantly, how will they make money.
We've all watched *Dragons' Den*; although Investors might be slightly less scary in reality, their focus isn't, and they are far from high-street banks.
The investor and venture capitalist communities naturally back the ideas that allow this recurring 'As A Service' payment model for obvious reasons.

If you sell stuff, you're only as good as the sales that day or month. If anything impacts your sales for whatever reason, do you have any real value as a business?
Especially in an online world.
However, if your sales or costs recur automatically, this enables far more accurate revenue projection and accurate forecasting of payback points and profit predictions. This data can be provided to Investors or buyers of start-ups as they become scale-ups.
The Life As A Service model also means that rather than having to 'buy', a customer needs to 'cancel' a service.
We often forget to cancel, making this a conscious calculation in future profit model predictions for the investor.
A very high number of subscriptions are actually rarely used. Often, it's also not that easy to cancel those applications that are coincidently very easy to set up in the first place. Try to cancel your chosen TV streaming service on your phone… yet you likely can't and need to access it via a PC.
In summary, not only is the transition from buy-now-pay-later to a Thing-As-A-Service lifestyle appealing to us, but it's also a no-brainer for Investors. Therefore, whatever wonderful solutions Innovators dream up, or we desire, it's likely it will arrive at our doors as a service, along with its monthly fee.

• • •

Reality For Us

As everything increases in cost and more things appear As A Service, this Life As A Service model will play a big role in the Future Of Us. We'll naturally embrace the convenience of these models, whether we like it or not.
They will bring flexibility and choice in place of contracts; increased competition to provide Digital Services will see prices drop; services will constantly evolve in a bid to lure us in or maintain our spend.

As explored, we can't have it all, so solutions will need to be brilliant to deserve our digital spending.

And, while we assess and review our spending, working out what's necessary versus what's just nice to have, there are a couple of red flags we need to look out for that are likely to have a significant impact in the medium- to long-term future.

The Evolution of Debt

One of the key areas of success of the Life As A Service model, besides the low monthly fees, is the absence of a contract. We can sign up safe in the knowledge we can cancel at any time, bringing comfort and a degree of control.

This is a great progression from previous credit options that saw us fund full prices and then pay monthly in a set term until the item was paid off – plus any interest, of course.

I won't disagree that the current credit options and debt levels are a toxic element of society. With the average household debt at £63,582 – which is around 107% of average earnings – it's no wonder debt so often results in stress-related illnesses, family breakups, crime, child poverty, gambling, and, sadly, suicide.

But is the Life As A Service model really any better?

Sure, in most cases, we can switch services off instantly.

But will we?

The national debt crisis would be easy to solve if it was simply a question of us saying no! This is a far bigger problem of, in most cases, people being able to maintain their lifestyles and desired standards of living. My call-out here is that this flexibility of Life As A Service will actually massively accelerate the problems ahead.

Today, we sign up for things far quicker than we probably would have done if they came with an annual cost or contract rather than a monthly rollover.

If annual costs were the case, we'd pause to give more careful consideration to whether we really need these services or not and if we can actually afford them.

So, while Things As A Service should resolve committed debt, I believe it just wears different clothes. In actuality, it will inevitably *increase* the cost of living and debt overall.

There May Be Trouble Ahead

Our recent history of the subprime housing market and credit crunch would suggest a similar pattern. The problem here, like then, is that the model is self-fuelling and creates a compounding problem.

The more outgoings we have, the more difficult it becomes to save for things in general – be it mortgage deposits, pension investments, cars, or holidays. This means we have become increasingly reliant on the Life As A Service model and eventually and quickly locked into it.

Dressed differently or not, debt is not a new problem. Surely, we can be sensible enough to retain control of our outgoings and take action to bring these increasing digital costs under control?

Well, overall, yes, we'd hope so. However, history also reminds us that responsibly managing our outgoings and affordability is not always a given across the board.

I'm not talking about you, personally. I'm talking about society in general.

Working Longer

The obvious impact and reality for many is that, as our lives become more expensive, our investments reduce and ownership of things becomes harder to reach. We will simply have to work longer to fund our Life As A Service.

And, if we think of the new Digital Technology we explored earlier, coupled with the changing landscape of work as technology allows us to work less but for longer and more flexibly, there are two mutually beneficial levers providing the answer.

If we look back over history, real change comes when several drivers collide. In our case here, several pieces and ingredients are falling into place that will result in significant changes in the Future Of Retirement ahead.

Wealth transfer and Divide

A further challenge of this trend, again talking at a societal level, is that not everyone will see these indicators of change and may be unable to review spending and investments in time or adapt to the new ways of working and learnings needed to stay relevant in their careers, or be able to work further into their retirement if needed.

A subtle but hugely impactful consequence of this will be that people simply eat into their savings faster and need to release equity from their property to maintain their Life As A Service model.

And while equity release is far from a new option – as pensions often underperform expectations and begin to fall out of lockstep with the current cost of living – Life As A Service will rapidly further fuel this option.

Over time, this will greatly reduce the generational wealth transfer in the form of inheritances that many people benefit from and, in many cases, bank on in their retirement planning.

Although no one *expects* an inheritance, the reality is that it's highly likely for many in some form or another. Our parents and grandparents were generations of homeowners, savers, and investors who then passed on these assets after death.

Over time, this pattern, combined with longer life expectancies, will significantly reduce the generational wealth transfer across society and drive the divide between those who have and those who have not.

To address this and maintain their share of our digital spending, banks will bring their own innovations into play to ensure they don't miss out.

Furthermore, as explored earlier, banks will provide longer-term mortgage options that allow us to retain a degree of asset ownership along the way, but for many, this will feel like a harder option and Life As A Service will likely win out, as we know we love the convenience and surely we can.... have it all?

I predict banks will also step into answering the digital spending challenge with improved spend-control applications as part of their bank account service offerings. There is a gap in the market currently; the banks are closer to the wider economic data and trends, and there is a huge prize for the bank that gets this right.

Digital Inclusion

The majority of those reading this will be scrolling through their banking apps or dusting off the pension prediction calculator while scratching their chins. This raises a question for me that goes beyond our personal circumstances.

How do we support wider society in terms of Digital Inclusion?

How do we support those who simply don't have the means or ability to access or fund many of these now essential Digital Solutions?

You could argue that a good number of the digital costs in our lives are luxuries or optional. However, a number of them are actually pretty essential for everyone.

Broadband is now considered a life-essential for many as it provides not only our communications and media but also our access to work, the wider jobs market, education, banking, shopping, and many social interactions. All of which come at a cost.

What's beyond these essentials that we should proactively provide to ensure everyone has an equal opportunity in the future?

In terms of work, how do we ensure every person has access to the technology needed to find a job and then the means to do their jobs remotely or in adapted workplace environments?

In education, how do we digitise every lesson and allow children all over the world access to a brilliant education remotely?

How do we allow children access to more advanced technologies to help prepare them for a Future Of Work we are yet to fully understand?

Access Without Barriers

For me, digital access should be without barriers.

Every child should be entitled to the same as everyone else; their learning is online, their socialisation is online, their hobbies and interests are online, and, whether we like it or not, their lives are online.

We can hope they simply disconnect and play outside with jumpers for goalposts, but I'm suggesting the sobering reality that we're fighting a pointless battle here. Planning for the future is a far more important use of our time.

If we look at some technologies that are likely to play a significant role in the future – specifically in areas such as AI, AR, and VR – the entry price point to access these types of applications is very high.

We have children interested in this who would love to explore these technologies further. Yet, even the most affluent would struggle to fund the expensive equipment required to access these services and solutions.

In our modern digital world, surely everyone has a right to an education? With what we now know of technology's power, surely these technologies, coupled with new innovations, can help bring the answers and support to a truly inclusive digital future?

But, if left unaddressed, these patterns will drive the Digital Divide further and present an unacceptable situation of digital exclusion and a wider divide.

'The future holds the power of inclusion but will exclude without intervention.'

We have enough information and evidence to call this out. Still, I'm also aware that this access to technology doesn't come for free and is too important to risk or rely on the gift of charity.

So, who's going to pay for an inclusive digital society in the Future Of Us?

• • •

Who's Going to Pay for the Future?

Well, as with every problem, innovation is never far behind.

First, as we start to make small actions or tough decisions in our current and future digital spending, carefully reviewing what we need, want, and can have in reality, we should also look for any tweaks or changes we can make to our future financial planning.

I'd be interested to know what you saved per month after cutting out some unnecessary or unknown digital spend. Tweet it to @FutureOfUs adding, #LifeAsAService and #FutureOfUs.

Second, while we review our spending, the costs of many of the solutions already in play will be driven down by increased competition. We will also see greater use of alternative funding models such as data trading and advertising.

In data trading, as I quoted earlier, 'if we can't see the product, we are the product'. As we become more aware of this and attitudes to data sharing evolve, will more people be happy to agree to trade their data to fund and maintain their digital lives?

Will we be given the option to knowingly share a level of our data in return for a free or discounted service?

Or will we choose to let the adverts continue to interrupt our digital experience in return for a free service over a paid one? Opinions suggest we will pay to drop the ads, but I think opinions will change over time as our focus moves from *convenience* to *cost*.

The Innovators, providers, and Investors of these solutions need to carefully consider which model they back and whether they have a point to pivot between the two models as the trends and realities evolve.

While these two options give us some manageable possibilities for many solutions, should we go bolder in our thinking here on alternative options to cover the costs?

Universal Digital Access

Are the growing costs of essential Digital Services and points around Digital Inclusion bringing together a call for a completely different approach?

Should we look to introduce a digital income for every person in the country? Perhaps a range of essential Digital Services funded by governments to provide inclusive digital access to all as we explored in the Story of Scout called *Universal Digital Access (UDA)*?

My proposal here is to introduce a social benefit for Digital Services that are funded by profits from efficiencies gained from Digital Services themselves. Not the taxpayer!

This UDA would be made available to anyone in the country to cover the cost of a range of basic Digital Solutions should their financial circumstances change or they don't have the means to fund these services themselves.

This would be part of a new Digital Inclusion policy in lieu of or in support of a current social benefit.

This would provide free access to various essential and social inclusion solutions discussed earlier, such as Internet access, communication applications, and education software.

Collectively, this would be a range of services to support someone looking for work, retraining, or accessing education and social interaction services. It would also provide funds for hardware or devices to access these essential Digital Solutions.

The funds would be provided in the form of a redeemable voucher instead of actual funds to ensure that they are not used for other things and that those in need actually get to use them.

This service would be means tested with certain elements interoperating with each other; for example, a family of four may have four vouchers for free Internet access, but they would only need one per household, so only one would be redeemed.

Social education applications may only apply within certain age ranges, and health monitoring applications may be provided free for those with relevant medical conditions while undergoing treatment or care.

Certain services may be made available at heavily discounted rates if considered useful but not essential.

This is similar to current Universal Basic Income (UBI) models that look to replace an income and are an alternative to a wage in part, or in full depending on the scheme in place.

These have been trialled and deployed in many cases across the world. The jury is still out on UBI overall as there is a clear division of opinions, but if we remind ourselves of the growing automation replacing jobs and the points I made around Digital Inclusion, many respected Futurists and leading Innovators suggest UBI will be the likely and possibly only end-game available.

I wouldn't rule UBI out, but maybe UDA is a good middle ground for now to ensure we stay connected and to connect the unconnected.

Who Actually Foots the Bill?

It's easy for us to consider innovations to solve digital access and affordability, but how can we also use digital innovations to fund a Universal Digital Access system? And how do we prevent it from becoming yet another burden to the taxpayer?

Of all the ways to spend our taxes, I'm sure most would be happy to support the cause of Digital Inclusion. However, ultimately, we aren't charities. I think there are more practical and appropriate ways to fund a Universal Digital Access system using innovative digital means.

We need to enable digital to fund digital.

I think we have three main options to explore.

First, remove cash altogether and make money 100% digital, using Blockchain technology or banks' clearing systems to fully digitise every single transaction. While I don't underestimate the work involved here, practically all the technology and processes already now exist to make this a reality. And when was the last time you went to a cash point?

The reason I suggest this is that each year HMRC estimate that £4.6bn is lost to tax evasion in the UK *(2018/19) and removing cash from the system and digitising every transaction using AI to recognise evasion would significantly reduce this. This would also help support the reduction of other cash-related crimes relating to money laundering and the drugs trade.

Second, is the current tax system fair? I might regret that one and wish I hadn't asked that... Sorry. But my point is that the principles of the tax system are inconsistent in many areas.

Take retail as an example. If you sell something in a shop, you pay tax on the profit you make and the business rates on the building you sell it in. However, if you sell something online, you only pay tax on the profit, not the building you sell it from (online still requires a building, warehouse, or office to work from).

More trade is conducted online than in physical stores these days. So, is the answer to swap taxation here completely to level the playing field? Also, how do we tax wider digital transactions carried out overseas?

While no one owns the Internet, if Governments around the globe can put regulations on the commercial property sector that it also doesn't own, why not tax a virtual business location rate as well, or instead?

Many of the largest tech organisations transact millions yet pay little tax in the countries these trades take place. Let's make this simple and agree a figure for every transaction is paid to the sovereign state for that transaction, a bit like VAT.

This could also then, in theory, subsidise many of the Life As A Services costs for those in need and not only bridge but close the Digital Inclusion issue.

Thirdly, while I have no issue with Innovators and Entrepreneurs enjoying the fruits of their labour, if we took the top ten wealthiest people in technology, a small dilution of their own individual personal wealth would have little impact on their lives but would massively impact the lives of many currently excluded. We should call it a Collective Digital Inclusion Wealth Tax.

We could also argue that UDA would actually positively extend the digital marketplace overall, bringing Digital Technology to many more people, who in turn and then learn and earn via digital access. So, while this might sound like a stealth tax, it could be mutually beneficial all around.

And finally, if we look at the business communities, many are already flying the flag in raising the Digital Inclusion agenda and closing the Digital Divide. Some organisations, especially the organisation I work for, are doing great work to make their services accessible to those in need by repurposing their old corporate devices into device-rehoming services that recondition the device, along with SIM card connectivity, into the hands of someone who couldn't normally afford them, but who can make great use of them.

Also, as corporate organisations refresh their employees' equipment to support their growing digital workplace needs, they also then battle with the e-waste this causes. Repurposing devices, therefore, feels like a mutually beneficial option and it's really great to see the positive work organisations such as mine are already doing.

Take a look at the great work organisations such as the Good Things Foundation are already doing in this space in supporting businesses and communities to address this critical cause: **www.goodthingsfoundation.org**

Overall, while it might be challenging to calculate the precise values of the above points, my point here is that we could look a little further at how digital could fund digital and open up the true possibility of access for all.

I'm sure there are people far better educated and more skilled Economists who can pick holes in my suggestions here. These people can probably guide and educate us on the likely realities or offer far better suggestions.

However, we have 689 million people worldwide living below the poverty line. Some working families rely on food banks, and millions are locked out of the workforce.

The growing wealth divide is denying tech savvy children access to the technologies they could use with ease and to great effect and technologies that are essential for their, and our, futures.

While technology quickly outpaces the awareness of Governments, organisations, and individuals worldwide, let's at least call this a start to begin the debate and discuss.

Digital Inclusion Is Societal Inclusion

We know this pattern, trend, and evolution might still be in its early stages, but the reality is that Life As A Service is here to stay.

You need no Futurist's insight to call out the growing evidence already around us and the projections this will likely have on societal transformation in the future.

Armed with this awareness, we all have a duty to raise the Digital Inclusion agenda whenever possible by ensuring we're working for and buying from organisations that place this high on their own agendas and by using your voice at the ballot box on Digital Inclusion policies.

Summary & Take Aways

- The cost of our lives is increasing at pace.

- The business of Life As A Service will set the model of how we buy and own things in the future; this is no coincidence.

- Ensuring we recognise this pattern and take action now is essential in our future, as we will live and work longer, spend more, and save less. Without awareness and a careful approach, we could become slaves to our futures.

- Digital Inclusion is social inclusion, and we need to ensure we all raise our voices for the cause and consider alternative options to fund our digital Lives As A Service in the Future Of Us.

*'Embrace the Now
Learn the How.'*

8
staying relevant in a digital age

'The illiterate of the 21st century will not be those that cannot read or write, but those who cannot learn, unlearn, and relearn.'
Alvin Toffler

Earlier I referenced the Dalai Lama's quote:

> 'The key to happiness is routine.'

But the very master of wisdom also said:

> 'Happiness is not something ready-made, it comes from your own actions.'

So, while we naturally crave the stability and certainty of routine, our awareness of the transformation and increasing pace underway – combined with the impacts and opportunities of new innovations – now calls for a need to push the call-to-action button for many of us.

Simply hoping we make it through the rest of our careers and into retirement without too much impact is fast becoming a very risky strategy.

We need to be masters of our own destinies and take action to increase our knowledge and skills to stay relevant, sane, and happy.

If we think about our current progress, our parents taught us to walk and talk, our education systems gave us lessons to read and write, and the world of work then equipped us with the vocational skills to do our jobs.

But who will take us to the next stage?

In a new digital world, we can't fall back on our parents or the educational systems that got us to this point. We can't bank on the experiences of our elders or expect our employers or governments to have all the answers.

With history as our evidence and the progress of today as our guide, allow me to share two quotes I constantly refer to as my own guides.

From the past...

> 'It's not the strongest of the species that survives, nor the most intelligent, but the one most responsive to change.'
> **Charles Darwin**

This is a timeless statement that grows more relevant every day. Should this be our poster title for the future revolution and everyone in it?

And from today...

'Observing the Future, for our Future, has never been more important in a time where change is inevitable but keeping up is a choice.'

These quotes may be close to 200 years apart, but when brought together, they summarise the time we now find ourselves in and the story of our time in the Future Of Us.

Transformation will happen regardless of whether we choose to keep up, and the future will hold little regard for your past achievements or future preferences.

Progress and evolution are a given; the roles we play and the path we take is our choice. The actions we take today and the progress we make will determine our tomorrow.

We will all be equal in the lifeboat, and simply put, the future, *our future*, is down to us. We all have the opportunity to be the early adopters, the new thinkers, and those taking the first-mover advantages.

It needs no former qualifications, just preparation, planning, action, and most importantly attitude.

'By failing to prepare, you are preparing to fail.'
Benjamin Franklin

But what are the practical steps and actions we need to take to stay relevant and ahead in the future? In this chapter, I will cover the key areas of relevance along with some practical suggestions, tips, and toolsets we can use moving forward.

Future Mindset

The biggest challenge with any discussions on digital, innovation, or the future is that many assume it's one for the techies, that it's automatically beyond their knowledge and grasp. Remember our quote of 'we're not technical, right?' And, sure, while the techies might naturally 'get it' faster than most, the future is not reserved just for them.

In fact, as we covered in Chapter 4, we'll all play an equally important role in building and shaping the future. Anyone can learn the skills needed to not only navigate the digital future but to prosper in it.

More than any string of academic skills, the right mindset, a positive attitude, and a heap of common sense are the vital ingredients needed for the future.

So, let's start with the two biggest challenges we naturally face when trying to get ourselves into the right mindset.

→ **Firstly**, I want you to drop your age! I want to level the playing field and reality of our relevance in the future. Years worked will be no barometer of relevant or useful knowledge in a rapidly changing world, nor will youth guarantee the energy and enthusiasm someone may bring to a role.

You are not too old, nor are you too young. Work of the future will be about attitude and adaptability, not age or experience.

In fact, as we can't be sure what really lies ahead, we should look at everything with the inquisitiveness and intrigue of a young child, asking the question of 'why' and 'how' to new the things we experience.

Don't give up your experiences or moral compass, but a little neoteny married with experience are strong ingredients Innovators around the world have. From Steve Jobs to Bill Gates to Elon Musk, they all really struggled to accept the norms in their fields from childhood to adulthood and constantly challenged the 'why?' with 'why not?'.

The traditional three phases of life (education, work, and retirement) are unlikely to remain the norm in the future.

We will work differently, longer, and more flexibly, and I want you to consider your life in chapters – with far more stages than our current traditions expect but with the acceptance that we may never actually write the final chapter.

Also, stop looking for the end. I spent years telling myself I'll be happy 'when' without looking at, or enjoying, what I already had and the process of learning new things. I then realised that each chapter is temporary, and the actions I take (or don't) are what write the next chapter.

The reality is the road is long, hopefully very long, so don't miss out on enjoying the chapters of your journey along the way.

→ **Secondly**, I want you to drop your previous education. There's no class in school or degree course for the skills we will need for the future. If you're lucky enough to have a great education and qualifications, awesome, but don't worry if not.

And don't assume any automatic preference if you do. A degree is no mark of intelligence; I know some spectacular idiots with degrees and some incredible minds without.

Now let's take a look at some of the key areas we should focus on as we build our development plans for the future.

The Human Factor – Us

I want you to consider yourself as a product (or a small business). You're designed from the lessons and experiences of your past, in theory, your CV.

But here, we're now going to build the elements of your future CV from a fresh awareness of the possibilities and opportunities moving forward.

I'm sure your CV currently reads really well; you got the job, right? But I'll challenge that the majority of CVs I receive mainly talk about the past, with little focus on the here and now and next to no reference of the persons future ambitions or focus.

I'll emphasise this with an example. Another motoring example, I'm afraid, but the motor industry is a great example of continuous improvement and constant innovation.

The example: We don't buy cars from twenty years ago just because they work well. Products and solutions evolve over time; they get better, and we want the new features and benefits that their continuous improvements brings.

Yet we take our educations, dive into work, and, for the majority of us, that's it. Other than a handful of courses that our employers send us on, we learn on the job and hope we stay relevant moving forward. Think of the cars made the year you started work; the improvements since then will be massive. What improvements have you made on yourself since that same time?

Employers, like consumers, want new features and benefits, and to this end, we should see ourselves as a continuously evolving product too. Just as with any product, it needs a research focus, a development plan, and a continuous improvement plan in the product: Roadmap of Us!

Evolve yourself. Develop and start to consider your next upgrade. Who you work for and with will change many times over your career; the one constant is *you*. Don't rely on a leader for a development plan or an organisation for a training course. Make it your responsibility and start your own development plan today.

'If you want to be wealthy and happy for the rest of your life, learn this lesson well. Learn to work harder on yourself than you do on your job.'
Jim Rohn

→ **Action:**

- Take a look at the development toolsets on page 254 onward. You can also find a downloadable copy at **www.futureofus.co.uk**

This starts the development plan of you. Throughout this chapter, we will look at some practical steps you can take to stay relevant in the Future Of YOU.

Beyond the Tech – *Your Superpowers*

The question of Robotics and advanced AI continues to raise its head in the form of talks of new solutions that will likely take over many jobs, as we explored earlier.

Sure, I don't doubt this will happen – and already is in several industries and roles – but for the majority of us, it will only take parts of our roles. This assistance will make our lives easier, but we will still be very much needed to work alongside Robotics and bring human skills to our roles.

Adaptability, logical thinking, and creativity will be among the highest desired skills in the future; these are skills that Robots may never be able to truly replicate and bring power to the people with them.

Adaptability – *Embracing Change*

The future will bring change we can't predict or control, and the very prospect of this will make many shiver. But fear not; through planning and preparation, we can learn to manage change and turn it into a far more positive experience or even opportunity.

New innovations will constantly appear in our roles, industries, and organisations that we'll have to respond and react quickly to, testing even the best-laid plans and preparations. Having the ability to adapt and embrace change, as we explored in Chapter 4, is something we need to prepare for.

I've placed the Managing Change model from that chapter at the very start of the development toolset on pages 254 onwards, with some guidance on the steps we can take at each stage of change. We should use this to help our thought process and to understand where we need to pivot and adjust our plans as change appears.

'The measure of intelligence is the ability to change.'
Albert Einstein

Building on Einstein's quote, one of the most important skills in the future will be to combine adaptability with embracing change. This is about not only managing change reactively but proactively to actively seek the opportunities it may bring.

Before we build our plans for change, we need to understand the need for change in the first place.

Is it because your job is at risk of automation or because you feel your skills and knowledge are falling behind? Are you stuck in a rut and looking at the next move in your career, or are you simply drowning in our increasingly complex digital world?

Become a Hypothetical Thinker

A great way to proactively embrace change is to consider the possibilities. The 'what if's'. Understanding why some innovations appear is sometimes obvious and common sense. However, sometimes, we might not immediately see the wider components in play.

Many innovations are quite logical, and you could ask why someone didn't think of them sooner. But how did people come up with these great ideas? What fuelled their thinking? It might have been a lightning bolt of inspiration, but it's more likely down to the possibilities of hypothetical thinking.

Not to give away all the Futurist's secrets here, but instead of focusing on a problem itself or the area of a product or process we are trying to improve, hypothetical thinking is about moving very quickly from accepting the realities of a situation to considering the 'what ifs' of the opportunities and risks.

Hypothetical thinking is the seed of the innovation process itself, encouraging thinking without limits. It starts with the wild possibilities of the 'what if's' and then filters down to the practical realities of the 'what now?' and 'what next?'.

Standing back from the wild ideas to see the sensible ones also helps you gain a view of the likely reality. I call this 'The Prediction of Possibles', and I use this in the early stages of my research to understand whether a new innovation will become more than just a neat gadget and become a life-impacting solution.

I work with a wide range of companies, helping them navigate Digital Transformation and innovation and Hypothetical thinking is often the missing ingredient in a company's current structure.

Who are the people who are going to focus on the 'what if's' of the current and future transformations? If we look at retail, I know many large organisations with very capable teams who were focused on attracting more customers yet while they did this, who was looking at the opportunities and risks from the growth and convenience of online sales? In the majority of cases, no one and this was the trend that took far more customers than they could ever attract elsewhere. This oversight caught so many long-established brands out.

Applying hypothetical thinking to our jobs and current situations helps us better understand the technologies in play that could bring about change and transformation in the future. This includes things that are already invented that might just need that collision of technologies to make it game-changing.

→ **Action:**

- What is transforming in your industry or your role right now? It might be new products, innovations, technologies, or simply something current that you don't fully understand. If in any doubt, take a look at the **Resource Checklist** in the **development toolset** on page 254 onward, to research *'what is the future of [your industry]'* or *'[your role]'* to find some ideas.

- From the above, next ask, what is the level of risk? Is it something you just need to be aware of, or might it transform everything completely?

- Apply Hypothetical Thinking throughout your research, consider the 'what if''s' and ask the 'why's'

Embrace Eternal Learning – Know Your Stuff
___

As the old saying goes, 'knowledge is power'. Although I'd say we should tweak this slightly to 'knowledge is confidence'. Think back to the '*I'm not technical*' quote in the **Understanding It All - Chapter 4**. It's a lack of confidence that often holds us back. But also know this quote from Microsoft's CEO Satya Nadella: *'We don't all need to be computer scientists to navigate the future.'*

This section is about taking steps to gain and build your wider knowledge of the topics you've chosen. You should now incorporate a new section in your CV titled '**current areas of focus/interest/learning**' with the goal of moving a few of these into the skills section of your CV over time.

→ **Action:**

- In the development toolset, take a look at the **Proactive Learning** and the **Resource Checklist** to identify and jot down two areas you would like to expand your learning on.
- *These tools are also available to download online at* **www.futureofus.co.uk**

Enhancing Current Skills

While you're researching new technologies and focusing your learning on the new skills you may need. Let's not forget the existing skills we use every day to do our jobs.

Take something you are already really good at, or should be good at, in your current job. Consider both soft and hard skills and look into how you can become either proficient or incredible at these.

Is it a level of additional learning, another qualification or accreditation, or just some wider insight and research to qualify what you already know or assume?

Don't forget the soft skills we might take for granted that help us work with others and bring a more personal approach to our roles and interactions, such as leadership, teamwork, negotiation, organisation, collaboration, and, most of all, creativity. These are skills that we naturally use every day but are skills that Robots and AI will likely never replace.

Our existing soft skills combined with a greater technical awareness of knowledge will result in an incredibly powerful combination.

→ **Action:**

- Do you have a current development plan for your day job? Pick it up, dust it down, call your boss, and ask them where you should be focusing your development, in their opinion.

- Use the **Proactive Learning** tool and look to the **CV Checklist,** to ensure you are rightly focusing and calling out your current skills and knowledge.

• • •

A New Approach to Learning

To be efficient with our time and learn while we manage our busy lives, I want you to break your learning down into manageable chunks: **Research, Learning New Skills,** and **Enhancing Current Skills.**

Research

Block off a few hours over the weeks ahead and start your research project. Make these bite-sized by breaking them up into thirty-minute slots on different days.

Pick one topic at a time; don't try to multitask. I'll come on to this shortly. Remove distractions and find a place to study. Really focus on this to make the best use of your time, and make sure you retain what you learn from the session in your notes or in the back of this book. Treat this as you would a course but by your rules and your time, but most of all, make it important.

Be resourceful. You literally have a world of information at your fingertips.

'You can learn everything you need for free.'
Elon Musk

Have a question? **Google** it. Scroll around a bit, the top ten results will likely try to sell you something, but you will learn to spot these.

Want to learn something? **YouTube** it. This is my go-to library of learning. Save the interesting and useful videos to a playlist so you can refer back to them later or watch them during your next learning session.

Stay informed. Build a **Flipboard** magazine from a mass of news sources that acts as your daily newspaper on practically any topic.

Hear expert opinions by listening to a **Podcast**. Search on Apple Music or Spotify to find an endless supply of interesting interviews on every conceivable topic. The world is full of experts only too happy to pass on their knowledge, opinions, and views on all manner of topics.

Start your more in-depth learning. Look into the world of MOOCs (Massive Open Online Courses) such as **Udemy** or **LinkedIn Learning** and sign up for a course. Invest in your development with a structured learning plan or course. Sites like these cater to a wide range of course options that are usually advertised in hours. Flag the ones you like the look of and keep checking in for offers and discounts; it's a competitive field.

'An investment in knowledge pays the best interest.'
Benjamin Franklin

Stay abreast of industry news and follow industry experts and thought leaders on **LinkedIn**. Fill your stream with useful and relevant regular feeds of posts and opinions from respected and recognised people in their field.

Understand the current mood and societal sentiment on **Twitter** by using solutions like **TweetDeck** to filter the info you want to see and avoid the scroll trap.

Start simple and keep your searches general. Ask questions like 'What is X?' or 'How does X work?' to learn the basics. Then moving on to 'What's the future of X?'

Then focus on industry topics or a specific field of interest. Maybe look at the inevitable changes in your own industry, job, or life. What are the drivers of change or the new innovations appearing? Research what you are currently experiencing. Arm yourself with knowledge and insight and use these resources to tackle the changes and situations head-on.

> *'You don't need to be smarter than everyone else, just better informed and prepared.'*

Rule nothing out in your future career... Within reason, of course. I'm not suggesting we could all retrain as doctors, but we should certainly consider how our new skills might turn into a new career for a future chapter of our lives. You're not too old, and yes, you do have enough time. I'll come back to this last point soon.

→ **Action:**

- Using one of your change topics, look at the **Resource Checklist** and consider some of the options to start your learning.

- Block out three 30-minute slots in your diary, but only use 20 minutes of each. Allow yourself 5 minutes on either side of the 20 to grab a drink or to pause for breath. Trying to immediately focus after a work call or wrestling the kids away to school won't work. Take five whenever you can.

Read

To complement the mass of free information online, also aim to read the words of the wise. Many of the greatest minds throughout history have put their thoughts, learnings, and advice down in words. They've shared the secrets to their success and the lessons learned along the way.

While we feel around the learning options online for what works and what doesn't, we are often missing out on whole libraries of tried and tested, concisely packaged guidance and advice from people we will likely never meet in our lives.

In books, we get decades of knowledge and experience condensed into a few hours of reading at our leisure. Books are a great way to expedite your learning and possibly the best return on your time and funds invested. Consider reading as a shortcut to your learning, with the pages holding the answers to many of life's exam questions.

Ask a colleague, your boss, your mentor or friend to offer a recommendation; we all have that go-to book that stays with us.

Find a quiet place, a dining table, a comfy chair or the bath, or put headphones on with an audiobook and go for a walk, but fall in love with reading regardless. It's the greatest distraction from your stresses of the day and the most amazing teacher of lessons you won't find elsewhere.

Also, if you don't already, get into the habit of reading a weekend broadsheet. Use this as a break from your phone's algorithmic heavy news streams. You'll find a good mix of national and international stories with different views and opinions on some of the wider stories driving broader societal transformations.

I find the FT Weekend has a great mix of articles, columnist views, and thought-provoking features. I also love the digital disconnect I get from laying the newspaper across the dining table at the weekend as I wade through it over a coffee.

→ **Action:**

- Pick up the book you bought during lockdown but didn't finish.

- Use a note app, a notebook, or a folded sheet of paper as a bookmark and jot down the main points you learn along the way. Keep these for every book you finish, as they act as a great refresher on the key points and lessons. You can use these as a summary to re-familiarise yourself with what you've read in seconds.

- Order two new books now. One on a topic in line with one of your **Proactive Learning** topics, and the other from a recommendation.
- Make one of the books an audiobook and head outside once a day for a thirty-minute walk to listen to it. You will finish roughly twenty books a year doing this.

Learn New Skills

If we think back to our school educations, while we might struggle to recall the last time we used algebra, our education provided us with a great foundation of literacy and arithmetic skills that form the common language for communications and commerce across the world today.

But now, with the constant advent of new technologies and the rapid digitisation of practically everything in our lives, we must evolve our learning for a new language of digital understanding.

The pace of progress is outstripping our current education system and the majority of Learning and Development departments across our organisations.

To stress, this is not a criticism but purely observations taken from my research and experience with my greater awareness of the pace of acceleration in play.

I'm sure both will eventually catch up, but until then, I don't state this to challenge anyone but to raise a personal call to action. We must personally address our current knowledge gaps to become digitally literate and relevant in the Future Of Us.

Again, it's down to us. No one will throw you a Life Buoy

The **Proactive Leaning** tool in the **Development Tool set** holds three key areas I want you to focus on throughout your research and learnings.

Digital Literacy: We need to better understand the technologies in play. What's the makeup of the common Digital Solutions in our lives and jobs? What do they do, how do they work at a basic level, and why are they useful?

A better understanding of the basics across several digital areas will help us better navigate the digital future. Is it an app, or is it 'in the cloud'? What is 'the cloud'? This might be one for your research right away.

Digital Commerce: Follow the money. Understanding the financial models of the Digital Services in play helps us understand the bigger digital picture and potential impacts overall.

Remember my quote, 'innovation that doesn't solve a problem is a gadget'? Well, gadgets don't make good business cases, but if something can improve a service with a financial gain or can help an organisation sell more stuff in our Life As A Service models, it will probably happen.

Holding this level of understanding will help us separate the services that will and the services that won't impact our lives. And remember, if you can't see the money, you are the money.

Technical skills: Having greater digital literacy overall will allow us the opportunity to ask whether we simply need to be aware of the basics of a particular digital solution or whether we need to take it further and learn new skills in order to stay relevant.

Some of our learning projects will be nothing more than a 'good to know'. Others will be more involved, and we will then progress from the research resources phase into the world of MOOCs to expand our learning.

→ **Action:**

- If you work for an organisation, reach out to your Learning & Development Team and ask what their plans are for Digital Literacy or Digital Competency. They may already have courses ready to go, or you might be able to help them find some appropriate content from your own research and explorations.

•••

Predict Change & Share

Use the power of Hypothetical Thinking coupled with your existing knowledge and new learnings to predict future trends or changes.

Many great innovations make perfect sense and really are innovation over invention. Apple, Samsung, Tesla, Uber and the like didn't invent the smartphone, GPS, motorcar, or taxi industry, yet the collision of very obvious technologies brought incredible innovation to our lives... Damn! Why didn't we think of them first?

As you progress in your learning, you will be met with lots of moments of revelation where you think of some really great ideas of how new technologies could solve problems in your working and daily life.

Of the new technologies you're learning about, what might happen as a result of their advent? Could it change your job, your organisation, or your relevance?

Why not write a blog or drop an internal memo up to your management team with any ideas you come up with that might be worth exploring? Trust me, no idea is a bad idea, and open suggestions from the people who do the work and solve the problems every day are never dismissed without careful review.

Are you the missing link that your business needs to take them forward into the digital future? They will likely welcome your ideas and input.

You Do Have Enough Time

So, we need to consider the lessons of the past, research, embrace the changes already underway, and keep our current skills sharp while learning new skills and reading more.

All this while managing our busy day jobs.

There are multiple plates spinning, incoming demands between back-to-back calls, and losing our long-standing and futile battle with the inbox. Not to mention then trying to catch up with family and children's sports clubs and activities.

All of this results in us barely ever having any time left at all, let alone free time to focus on ourselves.

The reality is it's so easy to deprioritise ourselves. As a result, we naturally put our jobs and families first, preferring to apologise to ourselves for what hasn't been done than to miss a deadline or disappoint others. It's human nature.

But the question is, are we really busy with things that count, or have we sleep-walked into some bad habits that are eating our time? Let's make this an opportunity to redress the balance and focus on the most important person in your life: You!

I'm sure, like me, you've read a heap of time management tips or books over the years, all advising you on ways to work smarter and be better organised. Some even offer new techniques or an application set to revolutionise your working week.

While they're useful, the problem is that we drift back to our old ways the second things get busy. We need to change our mindset rather than just deploy a tip or tools. We need to prioritise ourselves.

Your time is your most powerful asset. How you spend it is your biggest investment. See your time as a currency. You'll use some of this to learn and some to invest in contracted or self-employed work.

Firstly, I can sympathise with those now calling out, '*I simply don't have the time available*' and recall I often made it to the end of a busy workweek or day to then spend the evenings and weekends chasing household chores or kids' after-school clubs, often making it to the end feeling like I'd completed an endurance competition before slumping on the sofa to finally relax.

For many years, I thought I was officially the busiest man in the world until I looked at my screen-time app. Sure, I was busy. But I'd been spending over three hours a day on social media.

Now, let's take a look at the current spread of our time.

- ✓ There are **168** hours in the week.
- ✓ Let's assume you sleep **56** hours of these
- ✓ Your work contracts will vary but let's say it's **40** hours, but in truth, you give **5** more, totalling **45**
- ✓ **4** hours to exercise – I know… But we might, right?
- ✓ **7** hours having dinner with the family

You have **56** hours left.

You do have enough time.

I want you to invest one and a half hours from those additional working hours you're putting in and one and half hours from your 56 hours of free time. A total of three hours every week focused on you!

I want you to consider this a priority, not a luxury. I want you to prioritise yourself in your first step towards your relevance and future independence.

Challenge yourself firmly on this.

We wouldn't let our children skip school or miss their homework deadlines, so why are you not applying the same rules to your development and learning? Athletes constantly train, doctors learn new procedures and practices, and lawyers learn new laws and policies to stay relevant – we must continuously invest in ourselves, too.

Don't beat yourself up if one of two of these sessions gets taken with a drop-everything request from work or you have to pick up some family commitments. It happens. But be flexible and move them around as needed. Start with setting in a recurring placeholder in your work and personal diary.

Now challenge yourself and take a look at your screen-time app. Click on 'see all activity' and look at where your time is currently being spent. This might explain the dead leg while sitting on the toilet for hours or why the household jobs weren't getting done.

Instead, have your learning at hand. I have everything on my iPad and iPhone, and it helps me easily pick up my learning from anywhere at any time. Be that listening to an audiobook while walking the dog, sitting on the sofa, in the bath, at my desk, in a coffee shop, or waiting at the kids' sports clubs. Use your time wisely. To stress: I'm not staying stop social media, its fun right, just let's get a better balance.

→ **Action:**

- Take a look at your screen time – settings; screen time; see all activity. Then look at your average across social and entertainment. *Any advances on three hours a day?*

- Now work out where your three 30-minute personal time slots are going to be focused. The cat videos and TikTok dances will still be there. Set them in your personal diary with a notification 30 minutes before.

Next, I want you to focus on your work time. This will pay dividends by not only allowing you time to learn but also finding you more time to actually do your job.

Over time, we all fall into habits. While lockdown brought us new ways of working, it also brought us new habits of how we use our time. Sure, we're super-efficient now with our reduced travel and the fact we can be on back-to-back calls. But ask yourself this: Who got the travel time back, you or your employer? You might have gained a few more hours of sleep from not having to jump on early trains, and you might make it home for dinner on time more often, but the rest of the time, I'll guess you gave back to your employer. The majority of us did. We have sleep-walked into new habits that are not of real benefit to us. We protect our property and our money, but we don't protect our time. This is a great opportunity to check in and re-address the balance.

I want you to challenge yourself over the next two weeks as a trial on the below areas.

Do you need to be at this meeting?

Ask yourself whether all the meetings you're invited to are relevant. If you're not sure, ask. Have a template ready that you can cut and paste as a query reply. See the two I use below.

> 'Thanks for the invite. To ensure I can bring value to your meeting and to help me prepare, could you please provide some further context of the purpose of the meeting, the agenda of points we will cover, and the areas of input you require from me?'

Or

> 'Thanks for the invite but, unfortunately, I can't make it on this occasion. However, if you could provide a little further detail on the aims of the meeting and your expectations from me, I will look to review as soon as possible.'

Half of the people won't reply as they won't have time, and you might have simply been added to make the numbers up. Or they will reply to your message in-depth, and you can then accept, decline or reply accordingly.

Also, you may receive sufficient information back that either clarifies the purpose (so you can send the information instead of going) or propose a shorter meeting, as you are now fully briefed and should be able to resolve it quickly.

Everything in our lives is a block of thirty minutes to an hour, and many meetings could be half the time they are. Take that time back to invest in yourself.

Email – Your Biggest Waste of Time

Email is the worst tool in the corporate world and the biggest killer of your time, fact! It not only steals your time but, in most cases, prevents you from actually doing what you were hired to do and is a key cause of workplace anxiety.

I don't recall seeing the line in my job description that said, 'We expect you to try' – and I stress the word *try* – 'to keep up with an ever-growing inbox of emails, of which the majority will be of no benefit to you, and you will likely never reach the bottom of'.

Cold Calls

Salespeople don't get paid big bucks for fun. They will make all sorts of inventive attempts to get your time and attention and are very good at what they do.

Think of the time you wasted listening to a sales pitch or rambling introduction that is nine times out of ten of no benefit to you whatsoever, but you don't want to be rude, so you give your time away.

Stop right now.

Interrupt the next cold call that comes in immediately and ask them whether the call is a business or personal call.

Repeat this if they hold to a script. Then ask them their name and which organisation they are calling from. If it's not an organisation you deal with, explain it's a business line (you're the product/business, remember) and ask that they remove you from their calling list, ending with an equally as instant but polite goodbye, remember they are only doing their job.

Be blunt – Learn to Say No, and Fast

Be blunt and ruthless with your time. You must look at yourself as a business. Businesses that don't focus on their core functions go bust pretty quickly.

As above challenge everything that takes time up in your day moving forward.

Ask yourself: Is this email or call going to get me paid? Is it going to help meet my contractual objectives in any way? If yes, get on with it. If not, bin it and move on. Have those cut-and-paste replies ready to go.

Work out your hourly rate from your contracted hours and salary and figure out how much time and money you're wasting. Then, ask yourself this: Would a plumber or an electrician do a job for free? Would a lawyer dispense free advice, an accountant do your books as a favour, or a shop worker work an extra half day for no additional salary?

No, of course not. So why should you? Just because you're contracted against a salary, it's no different. Protect your time at all costs; you owe it to yourself.

If you don't value your time, neither will others. Stop giving it away for free.

Being so ruthless with your time will feel a little odd at first but keep a reminder in your diary or stick up a note in your office that says 'protect your time' as a reminder. After a few weeks, you will have set new, lasting habits, but keep those reminders nearby as it's so easy to slip back.

You Cannot Multitask* Be Present

Accept that you can't multitask. Don't fight it or believe it's actually possible. You *will* waste more time than you'll save by trying to multitask.

The reality is that we think we can just send a quick email while on a conference call or pick up a quick message in the evening while listening to the kids' playback their day. However, our brains are hardwired to focus on what is currently in our single focus at that time. Focus on the now and learn to be ruthless.

You'd be better off stopping the session you're only partly engaged in and politely dropping off if it's not relevant to you than half-listening while trying to multitask and then having to waste time trying to catch up later. If you're on a call you can multitask on, then yep you guessed it you didn't need to be on the call in the first place.

Eating lunch, biscuits, or going to the toilet while on a call are exceptions to the above rule, but don't forget to go on mute.

Furthermore, it can appear rude to send emails or chat messages while you're in a meeting – we wouldn't do this in face-to-face meetings. Yet, in our more remote worlds, with keyboards and phones now hidden below the camera screen, we've become serial multitaskers. Or so we think, between the echoes of *'sorry, could you just repeat that question, please?'*

→ **Action:**

- Build the polite templates I mentioned to query the meeting invites you're not clear on.

- Now look two weeks forward and send out the query emails to current invites as needed.

- Challenge the time of future meetings. Do you need thirty minutes, or would fifteen or twenty achieve the same? Or advise how long you can join for, e.g. *I can only make the first 15 mins*

- Set email catch-up time and focus purely on that in the time allocated. Do not open it again until your next email window, and switch off notifications.

- Consider a few hours, a day, or try a whole weekend without technology. Use some of the time to digitally disconnect. Buy a paper book or new paper as an alternative

• • •

Find Your People – The Vital Few

The Pareto principle states that for many outcomes, roughly 80% of consequences come from 20% of causes, also known as 'the law of the vital few'.

The Pareto principle has a natural phenomenon in that it can be applied to a wide range of cases and observations. In business management, we often quote the old adage that 80% of revenue comes from 20% of clients.

In sales and account teams, it's often quoted that 80% of self-generated sales and business come from 20% of the salespeople.

My observations suggest that this principle also fits well with those who focus on self-development and who see and acknowledge the transformation underway. These are the 20% that take a step to prepare for both the impacts and opportunities ahead. And, in line with the Pareto principle, let's call them…Us… You! The Vital Few.

The Vital Few are those who give that little bit more in their day jobs, build side hustles, take the step to go it alone, or simply strive to be the best at what they do. They sleep well in the knowledge they give it their all. The fact you are reading a book like this and have made it this far, means we are in good company, nice to meet you!

You! are also my toughest challenge, as all my advice to encourage you to take things a bit easier or give yourself some time back occasionally will be met with resistance by your very nature. You! will place yourself last in your pursuit and commitment to complete the task at hand and get the job done.

And, to be clear, this isn't to knock or bash the 80%; far from it. As we explored in earlier chapters, work is not the be-all and end-all for many. A large majority simply want to do a fair day's work for a fair day's pay, and we could argue that they're right and we're wrong.

But combined, we nevertheless form a great balanced team that will prevent us all from slipping into unhealthy overworking habits in the future.

The future holds great opportunities for the Vital Few, not purely by simply out-working everyone else, as you will naturally do, but by being the thought leaders and voices of change and transformation.

My ask is that you invest some of your natural energy and ambitions into future-proofing yourself. Work on not only staying relevant but leading the changes in your roles and organisations. This is your USP, the differentiator of you.

And finally, the most important part of the 20% club is that it's not about everyone striving for the top jobs, though many of you will naturally end up there. Think upwards; your management team and the directors you work with will have you in their sights as future talents and stars of the future. However, many of the 20% club find a degree of comfort, satisfaction, and reward from just doing what you do brilliantly and enjoying doing just that. Pick your position and play it well, really well, by continually investing in yourself.

Create a High-Value Network

You will know who the Vital Few are in your business, family, and circle of friends. These are the people you reach out to get stuff done or whose advice you take in regard to a project or problem you're working on.

My advice is to embrace your current network of like-minded people and actively reach out and connect with others to build a high-value network.

'Find people who fit your future, not your past.'
Many claimants

The fact is that successful people support others and learn from others. Losers focus on winners. Winners focus on winning and applaud the successes of others. Look for the people who celebrate others, those who click 'like', and those that offer positive encouragement to others in their careers and side hustles.

'You are the average of the five people you spend the most time with.'
Jim Rohn

If we are the average of the five people we spend the most time with, then let's make our wider networks up of hundreds of like-minded positive people to build a network of people with the same attitudes and motivations as you... Us!

As mentioned these people applauded others' successes, encourage all and are proud to boast of their friends' achievements. These are the people you need to and should be around.

Also, as we look to develop ourselves, be very aware that not everyone will be supportive of your development plans or side hustles. Sadly, some will scuff your ideas, and encouragement may be limited.

Great if you have an encouraging partner, parents, friend, or boss, but don't expect anyone other than yourself to be your cheerleader.

Be prepared to put in many hours in silence where people don't fully understand what you're doing. The reality is that some may be quietly envious that you've had the guts to go for it. Some will offer you their views of why it won't work, and some sadly will just silently hope you fail, which is, unfortunately, human nature.

Suppose you try and fail; congratulations. Most people will never even try. Reduce the time you spend with people who hold you back and increase time with those who can pull you forward.

> 'Stay away from negative people, they have a problem for every solution.'
> **Albert Einstein**

I didn't write this book for profit. You don't make money from writing a book on a niche topic aimed at only 20% as an audience. I wrote this book to reach and connect with the open-minded thinkers and Innovators of today who will collectively help build our Future Of Us... The Vital Few. You!

Let's connect at the LinkedIn group
https://www.linkedin.com/groups/12562045
or search 'the future of us' in LinkedIn
and start to build a network of people who will lead our tomorrows starting today.

> Let's make the *Vital Few* the *Vital Many* #VFVM

Get a Mentor

Imagine if you could travel back in time; what would you tell your younger self? What tips on life, education, finances, and work would you absolutely insist your younger self should take heed of? I have a long list, that's for sure.

While we sadly can't turn back time, we *can* use a pretty good alternative. We can take the advice of someone who has the experience to help through mentoring.

People tend to consider mentoring a work-related process, but this is usually because we look to the successful leaders or businesspeople we work with and want their advice on how to get there.

But don't restrict it to work.

Most of the brilliant advice I've taken over the years hasn't been specific to a job. It's been about attitude, focused learning, and common sense, and it's come from people who've ridden the waves of life ahead of me.

They share what they did, what they learnt, and what they'd do differently if they had their time again. Advice is usually universal, and we could all offer our younger selves a few pointers for sure if only we had the chance.

Well, here, we do.

Positive and successful people want to help and empower others. It's a Vital Few thing, as I mentioned, and they will likely be flattered you asked, and I bet only too willing to help you, a like-minded person.

Think about the people in your life right now that you can learn from or use as a sounding board. It might be a friend, parent, colleague, or leader. Ask them for some time. You'll be amazed by how generous and supportive people can be in helping others.

What's on your mind that they might be able to help you with?

'If you're the smartest person in the room, you're in the wrong room.'
Unknown

Many business leaders have been accredited with the quote. While it's difficult to know its true source, its echo is heard everywhere.

Think to your work colleagues. Think to your family and friends. We naturally gravitate toward interesting and intelligent people, people who we can learn from and those whose conversation stimulates us.

And again, don't simply measure intelligence by the role someone does or the qualifications they possess. Critical advice and learning can come from a broad range of people. You don't need to take every bit of advice, but it's better to have ten ideas than none.

The deal is, if you're asking someone for their support or wisdom, you follow these simple rules:

1) Be clear on what you want to talk to them about and put this in your initial ask-note or phone call

2) Keep the session short and respect their time; put in a 30-minute session and be done in 25.

3) You go to them. Make it super convenient for them and consider a video call if they aren't nearby.

4) If you do meet in person, you buy the coffee, lunch, or beers.

→ **Action:**

- In the **development toolset** section pages 254 onward, go to the **mentor network** tool. Here write down the three names of people you think you can learn from. Alongside each one, consider how you would approach them and write down some questions you would ask them.

- Become a mentor – are you a leader, business owner, parent, or friend who might be able to help others in reverse? Make the offer, which could be as casual as signing off your email or message with a footer of 'Let me know if I can help you further on this, I've some experience in that field.' Again, let's pull together to make the Vital Few into the Vital Many.

Don't Compete; Focus on You

Yes, you read it correctly. Stop competing immediately!

Hang on a minute, aren't we supposed to be ferociously competitive in our bravado-driven, chest-beating corporate worlds and careers?

Shouldn't we be constantly battling to take the lead on that crucial project, fighting for the top spot on the sales leaderboard, or getting ahead of the pack as we strive to climb the corporate career ladder?

Or maybe it's about being the most successful sibling or one-upping The Jones next door in your personal life.

Society has conditioned us to see competition as a key element in our plight for success. Movies tell us tales of winners, and businesses hire retired sports stars to speak at conferences and share rousing stories of wins and victories on the sports field.

All this is aiming to fuel our naturally competitive natures. It's part of who we are as a result, and for many, it makes perfect sense, right?

Well, that might be the case, but the natural reality might be quite different. Many of the brilliant sportspeople and very successful businesspeople I've met rarely compete with anyone but themselves.

They are driven in pursuit of a goal they've set their sights on or to be the best that they can be. You rarely hear them talking about beating their opponents; it's more about how they improved and pushed 'themselves' to achieve their vision. Being the best is a by-product of their relentless focus and determination. They are gracious in defeat, immediately focusing on how 'they' can improve. They are humbled by their respect for their fellow competitors.

They focus inwards, not outwards.

Competing against someone with these motivations is a waste of time. While you're wasting time focusing on them, they will be head-down, taking action to achieve their goals. It's unlikely they'll even notice you're there.

Many leaders may strongly disagree with me on this, and of course they will. You're part of 'their' focused goal; why have people just doing the norm when you can get them to compete and work far beyond their clocked and contracted hours, with the prize of a possible promotion at the end?

Many of the Vital Few will feel competition is still important beyond this for them, but this is often due to an upbringing that instils competition internally at an early age.

Be it to be the best sibling or the winner on the sports field. For many, it's quite a healthy thing, but for others, it's a horrible and unhealthy pressure. Parents can sometimes place unrealistic expectations on their children, often to do what they didn't.

I didn't experience this situation, thankfully. Although I did compete in sports to a high level as a child and loved it, I sadly saw through other children how the pressure to compete against others took the joy of sports away for many.

My focus was on continually improving myself. Become your own and only harshest critic.

Focusing on improving and celebrating your personal bests and marginal gains while dusting yourself down where you know you could improve is a far healthier and more realistic balance. If there was only one winner at work, it would be a lonely team. True winners and truly great leaders look at collective improvements and celebrate every success, toast every win and support and rebuild together.

Competition should be fun and placed in the right context and arena; don't let it distract you from your own goals. Focus on you!

→ **Action:**

- In the **development toolset** pages 254 onwards, take a look at the areas you are keen to learn more on and set your own deadlines and compete with yourself right here. Focus in, not out. Set your goal and personal stretch targets.

Build Your Brand – Beyond the CV

As you are the most important part of your future, you need to become a marketer of yourself and of your product. You need to be your biggest promoter.

Building your brand goes beyond your skills. If all things are equal in a battle for jobs or Gig Work, they are going to look for the passion and reason you do what you do. Don't be modest. Promote yourself; sell yourself until others sell you too.

Bu know your brand is not yours to decide at will, it's how others perceive you. But know that your brand is built from the actions you take.

Have an opinion, have a voice, and share your knowledge. Where appropriate, share your principles and values on a topic in your conversations, posts, and digital interactions. Your actions will build your brand. Not everyone will click 'like' or comment but trust me, they won't miss it.

We leave a digital footprint everywhere we go; the posts we write and the comments we make. Make yours around your theme and what you want to be known for.

Consider how your new learnings may complement your current brand or be part of building a new brand.

For some, it's an unconscious result of what they already naturally do. Are you someone that people come to for advice on a topic or if they need help? Has that area become part of your brand by default?

→ **Action:**

- Open your CV. Does it sell you? How might your new learnings build out your CV further?

- See download the **CV Checklist** from the **development toolset** and attach this to your CV as a point of comparison of the key points below.

How does your CV compare on these following points....

- **Know who you are:** Be confident that you're already pretty awesome, especially for the things you've achieved in your career. Let's have a bit more chests out and shoulders back for what we already do. Write down your top three strengths.

- **Know your field of focus:** Your skills. Be it academic, vocational, or self-focused learning. Write down how you would like to be introduced on a panel or podcast. Don't be shy here; sell yourself.

- **What's the story of how you got there:** Why are you credible; the years you've worked and the research you do – write down your experiences.

- **What are your current areas of development.** What areas are you currently up skilling on and why. Look where in your CV, could you add the line: **'My current areas of interest/focus/learning are.....'** and what would these areas be?

- **What you bring to the table:** What are you here for? This might be an interview, a sales pitch, or to support a project. Be clear on your why. 'I'm interested because...'

- **Why you do it:** Your passion – is this just a job for you, or does it mean more? There are two responses when you ask what someone does for a living. One is over very quickly; the other takes a while as you see the passion on their face appear.

- **Your unique qualities:** Why you? Brag and be your own cheerleader. If you do it right, others will join your cheerleading team. That's when you know you have truly built your brand.

Standing back from these questions, it looks a bit like an interview, right? Absolutely. These points not only shape your brand but should summarise the CV of you. Give the interviewers something to really work with to see the very best YOU!

• • •

Your Future Finances

While we prepare our skills and learn for the future of how we plan to earn a living, we must also balance our personal finances today.

As explored in the Life As A Service chapter, the cost of our lives is going to increase beyond the norms of rising energy costs, inflation, and interest rates. As we explored in the Life As A Service chapter, more and more of the things in our life will come attached with a cost to serve.

We must make it a priority to understand the true cost of our digital lives and to manage our lives As A Service.

The old saying goes, 'Money can't buy you happiness', and it's usually said by those with plenty of money. While I agree with the principles of the statement, as someone who built his own life from absolutely nothing, I'll also ask why we would want our finances to be an additional worry.

Trust me from experience, when you truly have nothing, you don't lie awake at night worrying about what learning courses you should be taking. You worry about how you're going to keep a roof over your head and food on the table.

And to this point, it isn't about being rich. Far from. It's about comfort and control. Financial comfort buys you control of your time. Time that then allows you to do whatever makes you happy. And if my predictions about the societal impacts of an un-considered Life As A Service trend come to fruition, this will result in more people being unable to do what they want versus what they have to do to fund their Life As A Service.

Doing something from a choice rather than out of necessity brings very different meanings, attitudes, and results. The psychological effects of this cannot be understated, making this advice the most important in this whole book.

Build a Control Plan

Get a hold of the finances, now!

Focusing on your skills is only half of the plan. Having the comfort of financial stability will be critical to your well-being in the future. Trust me on this one and apply both short- and long-term thinking.

Make some tough decisions about what stays and goes in your digital life today and pay close attention to this trend in the future. What's your salary versus your outgoings? Are you overspending? Do you know what all your outgoings are? What's necessary and what's not? Are you saving and investing into pensions for the future, or will you have to work at this same rate throughout your retirement?

Ask yourself, do you need the wine subscription or the flower service, and is buying clothes on finance *really* a good idea?

To be clear, I absolutely applaud every Innovator and Entrepreneur out there who has the guts and skills to deliver some of the incredible innovative digital businesses we'll see in the Future Of Us... however, not at the *expense* of us.

→ **Action:**

- Sit down and seriously attack the list of digital costs in yours and your families lives. Know it intimately. You might may not be popular after this exercise as you switch some things off some services and recut your cloth, but it's far better you do it now on the non-essentials before you have to cut back on the *actual* essentials.

As we explored in the Life As A Service chapter and to stress again: the current models of retirement will not fit into our future world unless we work to our dying days. And sure, I'm sure Governments will step in to help. But why would we leave it to chance? I say:

Plan for the worst and hope for the best.

This is not simply a new trend we can adapt to. Nor is this a guess or prediction, its already happening and will grow. In my opinion, the unprepared will pay a huge price in the future.

→ **Action:**

- Check your bank regularly – change bank cards or switch off direct debits and ask your bank to help. Be aware of every penny going out vs money going in.
- Create a spending and saving plan – do you need all your digital outgoings?
- Automate the basics – bills but also savings, and investments.
- Avoid item rental booms and credit cards as a gap filler.
- Create a big picture of your finances – forecast and budget. Consider your financial health. When could you retire? You might not want to now, you may

never want to, but having the option to is a nice comfort blanket to hold.

- Make good use of this fund to also insure your digital possessions or to replace other separate insurance policies you may have. This fund is a great way to insure a wide range of things from replacing a broken or damaged devices, or to cover the cost of an unexpected breakdown of a domestic appliance. I even use our fund to insure the health of our pets. I get that insurance is important but after many years of paying separate insurance policies against smaller Items and the disappointment and reality of long and confusing cover exclusions and clauses, overall I hadn't insurance much considering the premiums I'd paid. Here you decide what's covered and you bank the fund if not used. Trust me on this you will be quids in the long term.

This is not the 80s or 90s; resist the hype. You can't have it all unless you can pay for it all. Make the sacrifices now to insure your future. Your future self will thank you for it, trust me.

And finally, it's never too late.

Guess what?

You *do* have enough time.

My father lost everything in the mid-90s due to ill health, which I'd say was fuelled by the overworking and 'you can have it all' cultures of the 80s and 90s. We were homeless and didn't have a penny to our name. While most of his friends were looking forward to heading towards the final stages of their careers, my dad, while managing his recovery, was slowly starting to rebuild his life. With zero help from anyone, he rebuilt his life to a point that now allows him to retire comfortably in his 70s, all while founding a charity to support others in similar circumstances.

But guess what? When I asked him recently when he plans to retire, he said, '*Oh, not for a long time yet, son. I've got some big plans.*' #VFVM.

Consider Your Gig

Reflecting on your finances and looking to make savings is great, but we should also consider additional and diversified incomes. It's far easier to earn £10k extra a year than it is to try to save £10k a year.

Use the Gig Economy to not only soften the blow of rising costs of living but also to support your future life and retirement plans.

Look to use your existing or newly learnt skills to diversify your income streams. Look at the time saved and consider if this could be applied to a Gig opportunity. Don't worry if you can't see it yet. You might not need it at this point but may want to work on it as an option for retirement.

'Never rely on a single income.'
Warren Buffet

Regardless of whether you can retire, you, like my father, might not want to. Going from the stimulation and camaraderie of a work environment to the full switch-off of retirement isn't for everyone. After the long to-do list of jobs is done, many, given a choice, would step back into work – albeit at a gentler and more flexible pace.

As work becomes more flexible due to improved technologies and changing attitudes, employers will be able to retain skills without the full financial risk, and we will be able to work longer, either out of choice or necessity.

For many, Gig Work will be a more considered choice and a preferred option to diversify our incomes.

→ **Action:** Start your side hustle

- List your skills that could be Gig-ed out today. E.g., book editing, logo design, accounting, plumbing or DIY

- If you haven't already, now use the **proactive learning** tool and complete one for an area you would like to up skill on that may allow you a Gig role in the future. What was your dream job? With a world of information available and longer working timeframes, is now the time to give it a go?
- Think big! How can you use Gig Working to complement your new venture? Start small and think big.

• • •

Run, Jog, Rest, Repeat

So, we must learn new skills as we develop and evolve the Product of Us as well as look after our finances and take care of ourselves. All while managing our already very busy lives. But surely some more quotes from historical and future leaders are all we need to keep us motivated and on track, right?

Well, sadly not.

I'm realistic about our reality, and no number of quotes will provide the constant motivation needed to remain focused on everything.

So, I'm going to suggest an alternative. The reason I asked you to start a new notebook, a folder in your phone or laptop, or to put recurring diary slots in your calendar is that you will naturally get busy and distracted.

And while we start out with huge motivation, energy and good intentions, our motivations are often paused as life just kinda gets in the way. We get busy at work, family stuff takes over, and sometimes we just simply run out of energy.

Anyone who has signed up for a gym membership and used it weekly for months but then drifted off a bit and then stalled completely will know this feeling only too well.

Maintaining motivation for anything is very difficult, and most of us will naturally go through peaks and troughs in any aspect of investing in ourselves.

And now, here I'm supposed to offer some sage words that will allow you to remain focused and encourage you to continue… Well, instead, I'm going to offer you some more realistic advice; actively go with it!

We all have those moments of incredible motivation; we've heard a great speech, we've read a great book, or spoken to a great leader, family member, or friend who has empowered us to be a better us and encourage us to follow our dreams.

We immediately start to make plans and chart the actions needed to progress our dreams.

We sit a little more upright as we start to make plans, whether that's getting up an hour earlier and hitting the gym, signing up for a training course, researching our project online, buying the web domain for a new venture, or designing the logo for our future business.

We're unstoppable at this point. Sound familiar?

However, the reality is that **YOU** are not your job during its busy period when you start a big customer project that eats up all your free time.

YOU are not your partner, asking for support with the household duties.

YOU are not your children asking for your time or attention.

YOU are not your family and friends needing your support.

As life goes by, you can and naturally will put **YOU** last.

This is perfectly natural, and as our hectic lives play out, we sometimes wonder how the hell we made it to Friday, never mind if we had any time to focus on ourselves as we slump onto the sofa to pause for breath with a beer or glass of wine.

Now, again at this point, surely I should just offer you a word of encouragement or a positive quote from a great leader to help you stay focused to put **YOU** first, as **YOU** are the most important asset in your future.

staying relevant in a digital age

Well, I could try, and you could listen, but as covered here, our lives will naturally get in the way, and all our best-laid plans will hit a pause. But you're not alone. If everybody who holds a membership for your local gym turned up tomorrow morning, the car park would be a mess. The reality is that your life will get in the way, and you will naturally put others before **YOU**.

So instead, I'm going to offer you some more realistic advice here.

Run when you have the time and space to do so. Embrace your motivation when it's on a high, focus on **YOU** and make as much progress as you can.

Then as times get busy, move to a **Jog** as you look to your notes and adjust the plans, picking out some smaller tasks to do. Make them manageable and achievable, for example, reading five pages a day instead of ten.

And when the crazy times come, **Rest**. Don't allow yourself to completely stop your focus on **YOU**, but instead consider it a holiday and allow your focus to be elsewhere. The key here is to set yourself review points where you just check in on the saved to-do list. Don't do anything on it; just keep checking in to keep the plan and dream alive.

And when you are back in the zone, the plans are there, the to-do list of learning and progress is waiting, and you can restart and **Repeat** the process.

Know that investing in yourself is the most obvious thing to do but also the most difficult. Run, Jog, Rest, and Repeat until you reach your goal.

Some of the most significant achievements in history were the result of this process, with very few lucky enough to land their dreams on the first pass.

'If you get tired, learn to rest, not to quit.'
+Banksy

Take Aways & Points to consider

- Start today. Make today the start of a new chapter for you.

- No one else has the motivation or inclination other than you. No one will do it for you. No one will have the focus needed other than you, and to be fair, no one owes you a thing.

- As the world changes, so too should our skills. The key to successful adaptability is in embracing new learnings and evolving our skills.

- Dedicate time to your development. Be flexible but be clear it needs to happen. See it as homework you must do. Why would we put ourselves last? Find the time.

- Give it six months – set yourself a goal. It might be to learn a new skill or simply to know far more about something that's currently beyond your knowledge. Keep it simple and achievable; you can go big once you're in the rhythm of eternal learning.

- Keep going. Consistency wins but allow yourself to jog and jog and pause. Just make sure you keep picking the plan back up and keep the files safe and close to hand.

- There's no instruction book for the future. Focus on you! Hold the vision, use the tools, trust the process, and stick to the plan.

- … Oh, and again remember, you *do* have enough time.

'You Are Here'

epilogue

'We can only see a short distance ahead, but we can see plenty there that needs to be done.'
Alan Turing

While no one holds a crystal ball to know for certain what the future holds, with history as our guide, one thing we can be sure of is that it will bring change.

- **Change that**... makes sense, innovations that aid our lives, and which we embrace.
- **Change that**... confuses and concerns us, with initial disruptions that we must react to and learn to adapt, with complexities we may not initially fathom.
- **Change that**... will surprise and delight and that we'll wonder how we ever lived without.

Overall, these will be changes that make up the natural evolutions of us and our time in history.

And, if technology is the vehicle for change and innovation is its fuel, let's remember that we as a society become the driver of real change and our societal evolution.

One of my key aims in writing this book was to call out the drivers and levers of change that are already underway and why our time will likely be different from others. I wanted to demystify some unnecessary complexities and provide practical tips and advice on how we can navigate change. Most importantly, I wanted to give and empower a greater awareness, knowledge, and confidence to stay relevant in the Future Of Us.

We've explored...

The Story of Scout: A Futurist view of what might be possible with very little innovation as the Sci-Fi of today quickly becomes the Now-Fi of tomorrow.

Our Time In History: While some innovations feel uncomfortable or unrealistic, our history books act as a reminder and guide to rule nothing out and to pause to acknowledge the incredible progress we've already made.

The Pace of Change: Calling out the collective drivers leading to a rapidly increasing pace of change and likely accelerations that will impact our lives and careers.

Understanding It All: We explored how we can manage change and established the reality that we don't all need to become Computer Scientists to be relevant in the future.

Impacts on our Lives: How the digital future will affect how we work and how we earn.

Future Of Work: The role of technology in our working lives and how we can adapt to progressive technology transformations

LAAS (Life As A Service): A call-out to the rapidly increasing costs of our digital lives today and the need to keep this in close check for the future.

Staying Relevant: The main area of focus and the practical tips and tools on how we stay aware, informed, and educated for the future.

So, where next?

That Future Of Us starts today. It has no end date, and your relevance is in your gift.

The future needs you more than you know as technology advances, skills become scarcer, and opportunities arise. I will leave you with the following asks.

Stay curious: Keep that open mind that led you to read this book; keep considering the 'what if's' and asking the 'whys'.

Stay interested: Find your topics of interest, research them, and learn new things. Focus on the things that interest you.

Stay flexible but focused: You are your greatest investment ever. Invest in the product of you to continually evolve and make the time you deserve to do it. Make yourself a priority.

Stay balanced: Run when you can, Jog when you need to, and Rest when you must. You'll know when to do each but be ready to pick it up and Repeat again when you can and enjoy the odd tech sabbaticals to reset the balance as needed.

Stay brilliant: Focus on your current strengths and enhance them when you can. Learn new skills and become a positive voice of change and transformation in your role and life. Learn to surf the future; it's the source and will change your life.

Stay connected: Find like-minded people and spread the word; share your research, findings, and opinions so we can all learn from each other. Let's connect right now and make the Vital Few the Vital Many. #VFVM.

And most of all,
Stay relevant. The future is ours in the Future Of Us.

Digitally Yours,

Ant... and, of course, Scout
#VFVM

the end

...but the start of, the future of us

development toolset

Throughout the book, I've offered advice and actions on the practical steps needed to manage the disruption of change, increase our awareness to stay informed, and, where required or desired, up-skill in areas of interest.

In this section, I have consolidated the actions and provided tools we can use along with brief instructions on how to use each of them.

I want you to consider this as your personal future development plan. A plan that you can pick up and put down as required. A plan you can use at your pace as you allow yourself the chances to **Run**, **Jog**, and **Rest**, as we covered in Chapter 8. Remember, you do have enough time, and You are absolutely worth the investment.

The tools are available to download from the website **www.futureofus.co.uk** and I want you to store these along with your notes in a system that works for you, such as a notes application on your phone, One Drive, Google

Drive, Google Keep, OneNote, Evernote, or even a regular notebook. During your research and learning you will find some interesting stuff along the way and having everything stored somewhere you can quickly revisit it allows you to stay organised and, most importantly, to come and go as needed.

I want this to be your 'Go To' guide the next time you experience an uncomfortable transformation in your current role, or life, where technology and innovations are outpacing your knowledge and comfort levels. Or, when you simply want to look for the next stage of your learning, career development or the continuous improvement of YOU. There is no magic trick to maintaining your motivation or energy, it will come and go, we just need to be ready and organised to move with it.

Managing Change Reviewer
Reacting to unexpected or uncomfortable change

    Firstly, identify the challenge. What are the gradual or sudden changes that are causing concern? Note them down (do one for each challenge/concern). Secondly, map yourself on the curve. It's important you know your starting point. Thirdly, move down to the **Actions** and consider what you know today and where you need to focus either your research or learning. Regardless of where you mapped yourself, move left and right through the actions as required to complete your understanding.

    Finally, use the Resource Planner tool on the next pages to consider the methods you will use to gain greater insights or learn more about the challenge or the new skills you may require to either better manage the change or to stay relevant.

All images are also available to view and download at **www.futureofus.co.uk**

the future of us

Managing Change

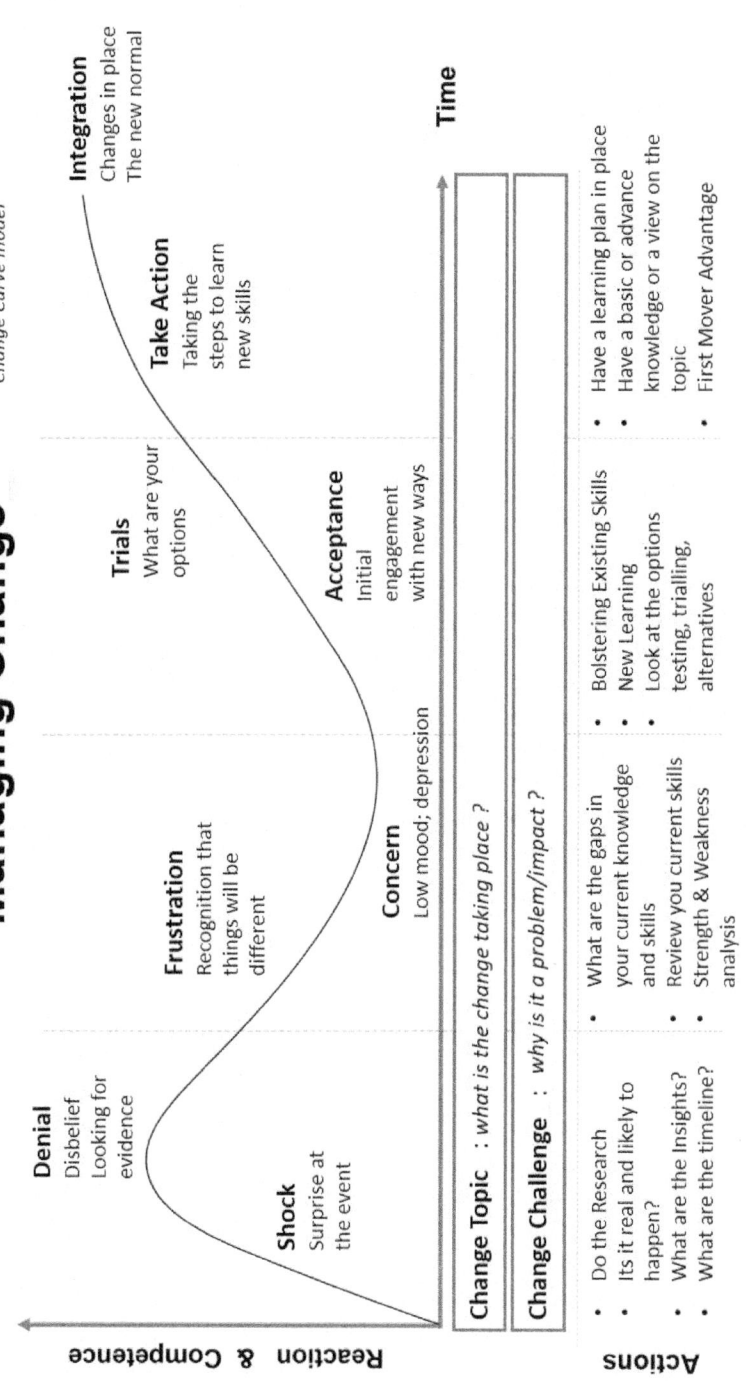

Based on the principles of the Kubler-Ross Change Curve model

Reaction & Competence ↑

- **Denial** — Disbelief, Looking for evidence
- **Shock** — Surprise at the event
- **Frustration** — Recognition that things will be different
- **Concern** — Low mood; depression
- **Acceptance** — Initial engagement with new ways
- **Trials** — What are your options
- **Take Action** — Taking the steps to learn new skills
- **Integration** — Changes in place, The new normal

Time →

Actions

Change Topic : *what is the change taking place?*

Change Challenge : *why is it a problem/impact?*

- Do the Research
- Its it real and likely to happen?
- What are the Insights?
- What are the timeline?

- What are the gaps in your current knowledge and skills
- Review you current skills
- Strength & Weakness analysis

- Bolstering Existing Skills
- New Learning
- Look at the options testing, trialling, alternatives

- Have a learning plan in place
- Have a basic or advance knowledge or a view on the topic
- First Mover Advantage

development toolset

Resource Planner
Our toolkit to research, stay informed, and to up-skill.

The best things in life are free! Most of the information you need to research and learn more is freely available on the Internet, whether using the Change Cycle Reviewer or increasing your knowledge and skills through the Proactive Learning Planner. Use this tool to give yourself a range of options to learn more. No matter how complex or rare the topic might be, or whether it is work- or hobby-related. I will bet somebody somewhere will have written a paper or recorded a video clip telling you what it is, how it works, and what might happen in the future of that topic.

In the applications you use to research, store findings or the pages of interest using a 'save article' or 'add to a favourites tab/option', build a playlist or saved list, or simply copy the URL to the note's application on your phone. You will find stuff you want to read later, and again, it's important to have this in a single or limited location. When I come to do my thirty-minute development slots, I know where everything is and simply pick up where I left off.

All images are also available to view and download at www.futureofus.co.uk

the future of us

resources checklist

The Need	Resource	Points to consider
Have a question	Internet Search **Google, Bing, Safari**	Search.... - What is X ? - How does X work ? - How does X make money? - What is the future of X?
Learn something New	You Tube, Vimeo,	Tweak your searches and look for the new number view, aim for the content with high views. The quality is likely to be higher. This is my go-to library of learning and I have a play list of every area I'm researching
Staying Informed	Flipboard	Register for an account and take a shot at Flipping stories into New Magazines, start a new magazine for every topic of interest.
Hear from the Experts	Podcasts: **Spotify, Apple Music**	Whichever streaming apps you use, take a look at the search and category options and spend some time looking for the experts in your fields of interest and subscribe to the streams.
Progress your learning	On Line Courses: **Udemy, LinkedIn Learning**	Look into the world of MOOCs (Massive Open Online Courses) Find a course of interest and invest in your development with a structured learning plan or course. Sites like these cater to a wide range of course options that are usually advertised in hours need to complete. Flag the ones you like the look of and keep checking in for offers and discounts; it's a competitive field.
What's happened in your industry	LinkedIn	Set up an account if not already on **LinkedIn** and start my reaching out to the people you already know if your industry. Then search for the experts you know. Let the AI in the system then find and make suggestions to you. And as you build your network, look for the mutual connections. It's a big but small world and while it has become a bit challenge by people selling stuff, its still remains an excellent networking tool for pretty much every industry
Current Mood	Twitter	Love it or hate it Twitter is still the fastest news feed I the world. Whether its hearing from leader and experts across industry or hearing news stories break first via the crowd, use Twitter and solutions like **TweetDeck** to stay ahead of the trends and close to wider social sentiment on topics of interest

development toolset

Proactive Learning
For learning and up-skilling

Whether it's unexpected change, a specific topic you want to learn more about, or an upcoming technology that's continually appearing in your role or life, or a term that keeps coming up and flying over your head as the conversations drift away from you. This planner is aimed to provide a very simply starting point to help you learn more. Again, this could be to simply have a better understanding on the topic, or it could be the start of more in-depth learning and up skilling.

Firstly, note down the topic you wish to learn more about, Secondly, work through the questions and use the Resource Planner to learn more about the topic. Finally, as you learn more you will form an opinion, or back someone else's, again this might be one to revisit as you learn more but knowing enough to have an opinion and view is a deadly combination and moves you into a new confidence and a totally different conversation.

Don't rush the answers; keep these questions in mind and keep using your thirty-minute development slots to keep revisiting them.

And to add a note of caution, there will always be someone who knows more than you or challenges what know. Some will be constructive, others not so, and some might just take great delight in telling you they know more than you. Some might become mentors who you can learn more from; others will be the people you would rather pull the fire alarm than listen to. Use your judgement to decide, but don't let them dim your confidence. As we explored in Chapter 8, not everyone will support your plans and dreams; look for the Vital Few.

All images are also available to view and download at www.futureofus.co.uk

proactive learning

Topic :

Focus Areas	Question	Your Findings	Resource Tool
Digital Literacy	What is it ?	Could you explain this topic to someone in simple terms?	Which tools could help you learn more
Digital Commerce	How does it work commercially?	Remember the quote 'innovation that doesn't solve a problem is a gadget' if it doesn't make someone money, its perhaps not such a big problem	Which tools could help you learn more
Societal impact	How and why might this change how people live and work?	What are the wider impacts and knock on consequences of this?	Which tools could help you learn more
Your Opinion	What do you think?	As you learn more, consider your own view. Is it real or over hyped, is it a career or business opportunity?	Do you share it? Twitter, LinkedIn ...
Tech Skill	What is your skill level on this topic?	Interested? Aware? Knowledgeable? Recognised? Expert?	Is this the topic you should take an online course in?

the future of us

Mentor Network
Finding the Vital Few

As we explored in Chapter 8, we need to find our people. For me, mentoring is the very best source of advice and guidance for all things in life. If a book is a playback of someone's experience and life lessons, mentoring sessions are the next step up. Reading all the books and blogs is great, but there's no substitute for asking someone who has lived and breathed the topic for many years for their candid opinion over coffee. It's priceless.

Work through this tool and give thoughts to who you know and who you could reach out to, to help you learn more on your key areas of interest, or general guidance and advice.

All images are also available to view and download at **www.futureofus.co.uk**

the future of us

mentor network

Area of Advice	Who? Who immediately comes to mind on this topic?	Approach How do you plan to approach them? a call, message, email, or in response to a social post asking to learn more	Questions to ask Prepare a very clear ask on what you need their help on.
Learning		e.g. I understand you're an expert in the field of X, could I possibly grab 20 mins of your time to learn more on the subject ?	ask the questions you still have gaps on. Or e.g. I'm looking to increase my knowledge in X, from your experience how is it best to approach this?
Research		e.g. I'm currently doing some research in X, could I trouble you for 20 mins to check my understanding on a few points?	(Be specific where you can and as your knowledge increases ask the precise questions you need clarity on)
Career		e.g. I'm looking for the next step in my career and keen to take your views on X, could trouble you for 20 mins to learn more about it? e.g. I would welcome your advice and guidance on how I can progress/develop into this field.	e.g. What skills or experience might I need to progress into this field e.g. Could you give me some honest feedback on my CV? e.g. What's the one skill you wished you'd learned sooner? And why ?
Other	Mentoring may start with career-related topics but often strays and experience and wisdom are priceless on any front, from pensions, holidays or great reads. The Vital Few will help wherever they can.		

development toolset

CV Check List

If you're reading this for the first time, let's consider this a chance to upgrade or refresh your CV. If you're reading this for the second, third, or fourth time, welcome back, friend. Let me guess, you're dusting down the CV, either from frustration at something in your day job or as the itch to progress your career appears, or you're looking for a complete change of job and lifestyle completely.

Here we will walk through the branding of YOU, in a digital world where qualifications appear to matter less and your attitude, self-development and practical industry knowledge means more. A CV is fundamentally a chance to really sell yourself. A time to leave your modesty at the door, you need to really brag about what you've done or are doing and put across the best version of yourself. Only the Vital Few are very good and this. Don't miss this chance to make it clear you're in that camp and are taking ownership and actions personally to stay relevant in the Future Of Us.

Aim to give the interview that line to explore in your CV My current areas of focus, interest and learning are…'

All images are also available to view and download at **www.futureofus.co.uk**

CV checklist

Area	Action	Notes
Know who you are	Write down your key strengths and list your achievements.	
Know your field of Focus	Your knowledge and experience.	
What's the story so far	Summarise your history but keep it short and expand on the very recent and detail the here and now.	
Your current development areas	What you are currently learning more about?	
Why you do it	Why are you passionate about this?	
Future Focus	My current areas of focus / Interest / learning are....	
Why You	Brag, boast, or be slightly modest, but make sure you bring all the above together to let them know you're in the Vital Few, as interviewers, we know when we meet you.	

The Challenge

Regardless of when you are reading this section, I want you to use this moment to set yourself two challenges.

Firstly, choose two proactive learning topics for the next six months. Consider your job, your hobbies, or just something that keeps coming up that you don't understand. If unsure, flip to page 85 and take a look at some of the Mega Trends I covered and choose two of these.

Secondly, reach out to a new mentor. Refer back to page 235 as a reminder of how it works and remember to be super clear on your ask of what you want their help with. Get the tea and cake ready and enjoy the process and conversations.

No matter how busy you are, you do have enough time for this, find the time in your diary and start the investment in YOU today!

let's connect

LinkedIn - https://uk.linkedin.com/in/antmorse

LinkedIn group https://www.linkedin.com/groups/12562045

Twitter - https://twitter.com/AntMorseUK

Instagram - https://www.instagram.com/antmorse/

YouTube - https://www.youtube.com/@thefutureofus678

Internet – www.futureofus.co.uk

Printed in Great Britain
by Amazon